IZZI HOWELL

AND

SONYA NEWLAND

THE BRIGHT BODY BOOK

DISCOVER THE HUMAN BODY IN GLORIOUS TECHNICOLOUR

WAYLAND
www.waylandbooks.co.uk

Contents

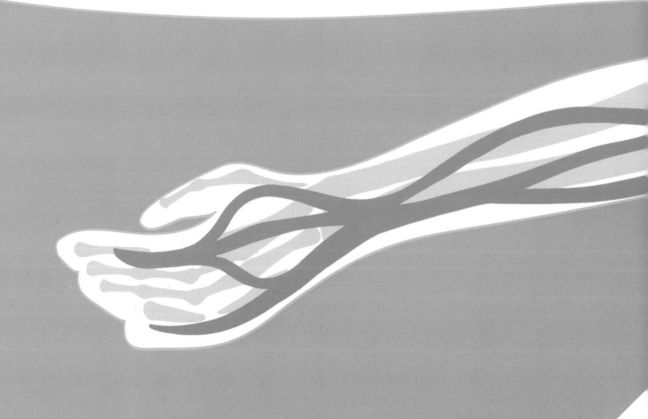

YOUR
BRIGHT
BODY

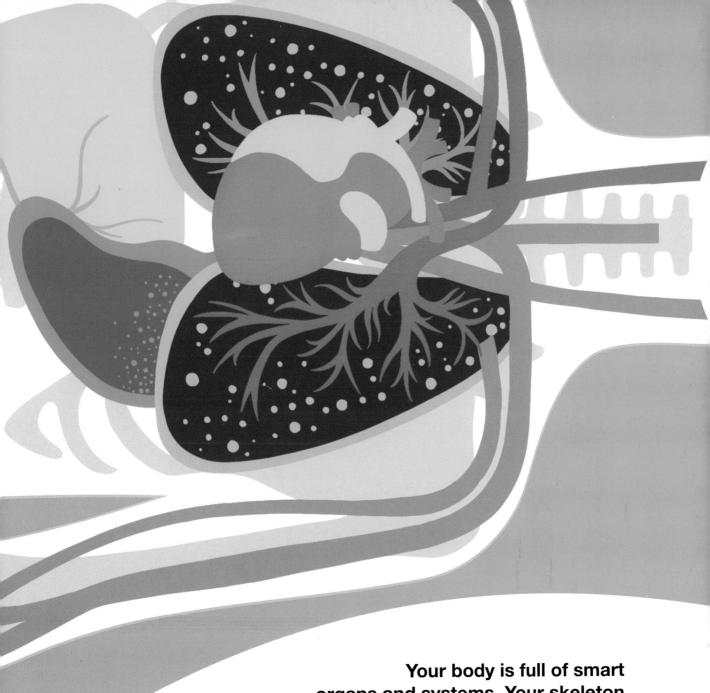

Your body is full of smart organs and systems. Your skeleton and muscles are your support structure; your circulatory system is a delivery service; your brain and nervous system are a communication network; the senses are identification devices; your digestive system helps you to refuel; and the reproductive system can create new life.

Discover how all these clever systems work with *The Bright Body Book*.

THE SKELETON AND MUSCLES

There are 206 bones in an adult's skeleton. Some support the body, while others protect the organs or allow you to move. Bones are also where blood is made and minerals are stored.

Long bones, such as the ones in your arms and legs, support your weight and help you move.

Other bones have irregular shapes. These include the pelvis and vertebrae.

Flat bones, such as your ribs and sternum, protect your organs.

Small, round sesamoid bones work with and protect the tendons in your hands, knees and feet.

Short bones are roughly cube-shaped. They are found in the wrists and ankles.

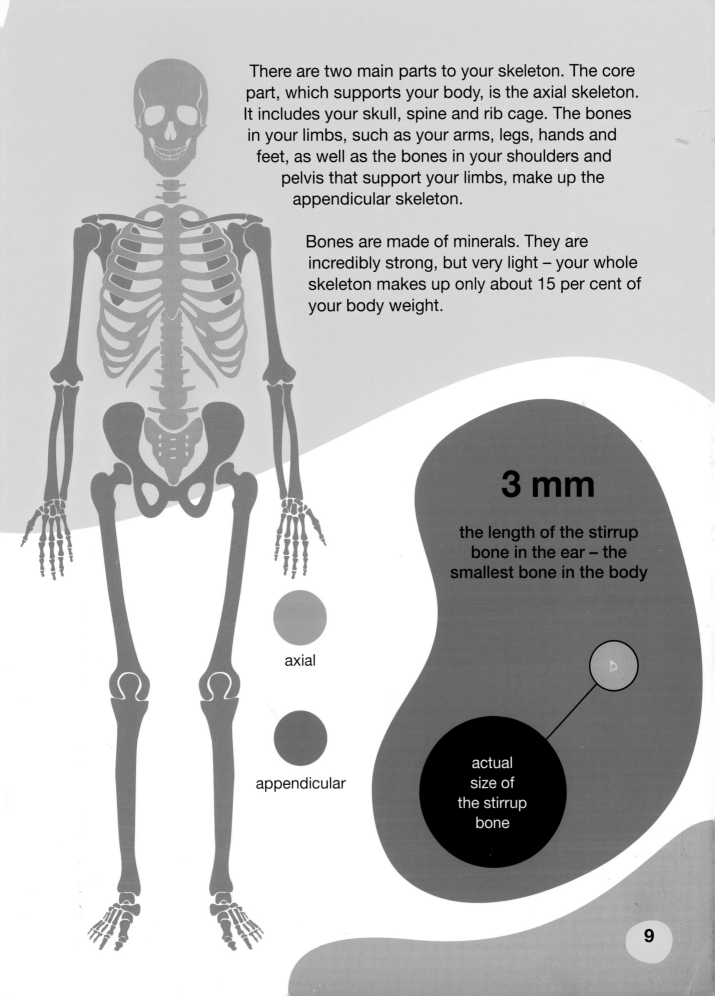

There are two main parts to your skeleton. The core part, which supports your body, is the axial skeleton. It includes your skull, spine and rib cage. The bones in your limbs, such as your arms, legs, hands and feet, as well as the bones in your shoulders and pelvis that support your limbs, make up the appendicular skeleton.

Bones are made of minerals. They are incredibly strong, but very light – your whole skeleton makes up only about 15 per cent of your body weight.

3 mm

the length of the stirrup bone in the ear – the smallest bone in the body

axial

appendicular

actual size of the stirrup bone

Growing bones

At birth, a baby has more than 300 bones. Some are made of a strong tissue called cartilage. Over time, these bones join together to get bigger, longer and stronger.

bone

cartilage

Many bones in the skull are not joined at birth. This makes the head softer so it's easier for a baby to be born.

The ears and the bottom part of the nose remain cartilage. That's why you can wobble them about.

Some bones in the arms and legs aren't fused at birth, so they can grow more easily.

Kneecaps only harden into bone at around the age of three.

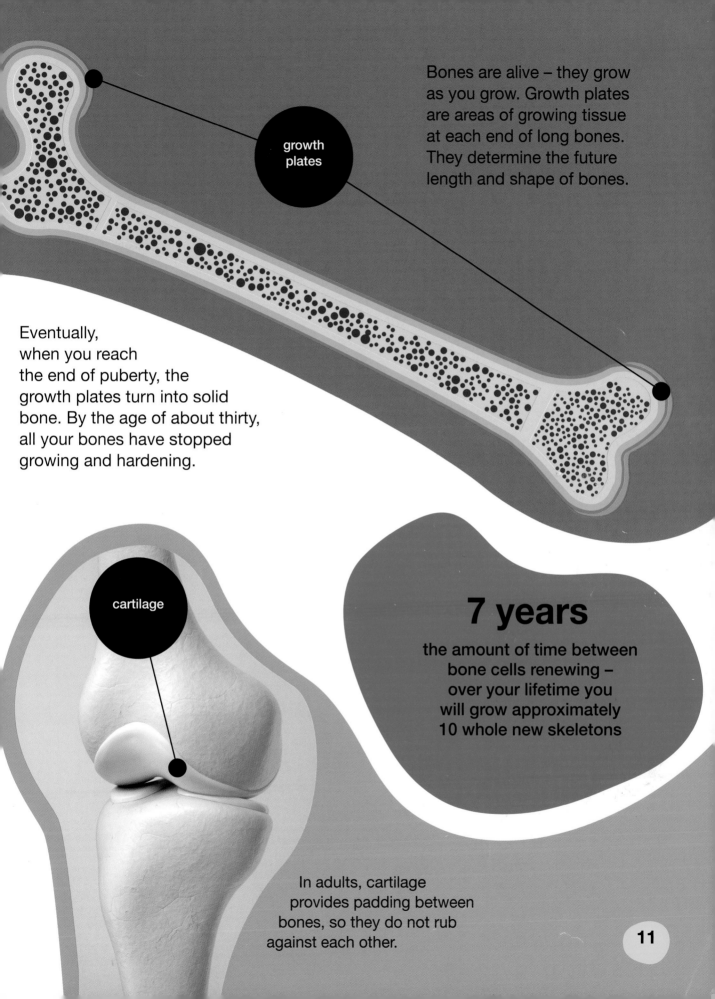

growth
plates

Bones are alive – they grow as you grow. Growth plates are areas of growing tissue at each end of long bones. They determine the future length and shape of bones.

Eventually, when you reach the end of puberty, the growth plates turn into solid bone. By the age of about thirty, all your bones have stopped growing and hardening.

cartilage

7 years

the amount of time between bone cells renewing – over your lifetime you will grow approximately 10 whole new skeletons

In adults, cartilage provides padding between bones, so they do not rub against each other.

Inside bones

Bones also perform the important task of making blood. This happens in the bone marrow, deep inside long bones such as the ones in your arms and legs.

The outside of the bone is covered in a thin membrane that contains veins and arteries. These carry everything your bones need to keep them healthy.

Next is a layer of smooth, hard, compact bone.

Yellow bone marrow, where fat is stored, runs through long bones.

Bone marrow is a soft, jelly-like substance. It is here, in the bone marrow, that adult stem cells are made. Adult stem cells can develop into different types of blood cells – red, white or platelets.

200 billion

the number of new red blood cells your bone marrow makes every day

The inside is made of spongy bone with a honeycomb structure. This makes your bones light but strong.

This microscope image shows bone marrow and blood cells.

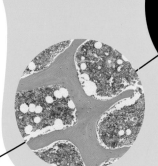

Red bone marrow, where blood cells are created, fills the spaces in the spongy bone.

Different blood cells have different tasks. Red blood cells carry oxygen around your body. White blood cells fight infection. Platelets help your blood to clot, to stop you bleeding when you're hurt. All these types of blood cell are constantly dying, so they need to be replaced all the time.

The skull and ribs

Bones such as the skull and ribs are designed to protect your organs. Without this strong outer frame, important organs would be easily damaged.

The skull is made up of several bones that fit closely together. Cranial bones protect your brain. Facial bones give your face its structure.

Two parietal bones form the top and sides of the skull.

The occipital bone joins with the top of the spine.

Eye sockets hold the eyes in place.

The facial bones are at the front of the skull.

The temporal bones form the lower sides of the skull.

The jawbone (mandible) is the only skull bone that can move.

22

the number of bones in the skull – 8 in the cranium and 14 in the face

Your heart and lungs are protected by a frame of bones called the rib cage. This is made up of twelve pairs of ribs, which are all joined to the spine at the back.

The sternum is a strong, flat bone at the front of your chest. The top seven pairs of ribs attach to this at the front.

The next three pairs are connected to the ribs above them with cartilage.

The last two pairs of ribs are 'floating ribs'. They don't attach to anything at the front.

The spine

The spine is a long column of bones down your back. It supports your head and body, protects your spinal cord and allows you to move.

The spine is made up of thirty-three bones, called vertebrae. Between the vertebrae are discs of strong, flexible cartilage surrounding a soft core. The discs hold the vertebrae together and act as shock absorbers.

Below this are twelve bones called the thoracic vertebrae.

Each vertebra has a strong round body that supports most of the weight. The spinal cord runs through a hole in the middle.

The top seven vertebrae are in your neck and are called the cervical vertebrae.

hole for
spinal cord

body

The spinal cord is an important part of your nervous system. It is a collection of nerves connected to other nerves around your body. Instructions on how and when to move are sent around this system.

Damage to the spine (shown in red here) can cause paralysis. If messages can't get through via the nerves, the body is unable to move.

The bottom four vertebrae are fused to make the coccyx.

Five lower vertebrae make up the lumbar spine. These are bigger than the other vertebrae because they need to support more weight.

The sacrum is made up of five vertebrae fused together.

3

the number of curves in your back – these make your spine so flexible that it can form two-thirds of a perfect circle when bent

Joints

A joint is the place where two or more bones meet. There are more than 200 joints in the human body. Without them, you couldn't run, jump, swim, kick, bend or twist.

There are three types of joint:
- fibrous joints cannot move (e.g. skull joints)
- cartilaginous joints can move a little (e.g. spinal joints)
- synovial joints can move freely (e.g. arms and legs)

Different synovial joints move in different ways.

pivot joint (e.g. neck and spine)

ball and socket joint (e.g. hip and shoulder)

saddle joint (e.g. thumbs)

hinge joint (e.g. knee and elbow)

The knee joint is the largest and most complicated joint in the human body. It has to be strong enough to support the weight of your upper body. It helps your lower leg move and has to absorb a lot of impact.

femur (thigh bone)

A liquid called synovial fluid keeps joints moving smoothly.

The patella (knee cap) protects the knee and joins the thigh muscles to the tibia.

tibia (shin bone)

29

the number of major joints in the hand

fibula (calf bone)

Bone breaks and diseases

Although bones are very strong, they can still break. However, like almost any other body part that gets broken or damaged, bones can mend.

2
the average number of bones people break in their lives – the collarbone is the most commonly broken bone

After a few days, bone fibres and cartilage begin to form in the break of the bone.

After two or three months, hard bone has formed and the break is completely healed.

clot

soft bone

bone fibres

When a bone fractures (breaks), blood leaks from the blood vessels and forms a blood clot.

Within three weeks, soft bone begins to grow around the bone fibres.

Sometimes bones break because they are not as strong as they should be. Brittle bone disease is an illness that makes bones very fragile. People who have this disease are usually born with it. They may suffer many broken bones throughout their lives.

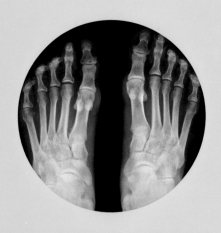

Doctors use X-rays to see inside the human body. This helps them to find broken bones.

Arthritis is a disease that causes swelling in the joints between bones. There are two different types of arthritis:

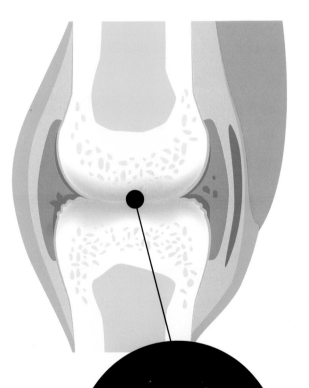

Osteoarthritis is when the cartilage wears down, so the bones rub together.

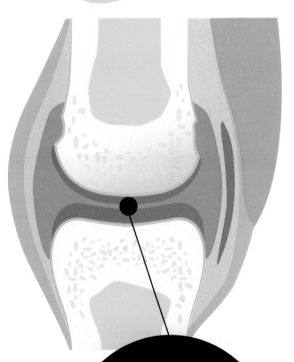

Rheumatoid arthritis is when the joints become swollen, which may cause the bone to wear away.

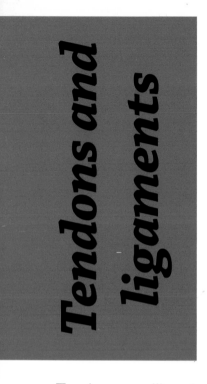

Tendons and ligaments

Tendons and ligaments are both types of connective tissue. Tendons connect muscles with bones to help them move. Ligaments hold the bones together in joints.

4,000

the number of tendons in the body

Tendons are like strong, rubbery ropes. When you flex a muscle, it pulls on the tendon. The tendon pulls on the bone it's attached to and makes it move.

Your fingers are incredibly strong, but they don't look muscly. That's because the muscles that control your fingers are actually in your arm. They are attached to your finger bones by long tendons.

tendon

nerve

artery

ligament

There are twenty-seven bones in your hand, held in place by ligaments.

Bones, joints, muscles and tendons all need to stay in the right place. That's where ligaments come in. These strong bands of tissue stop bones wobbling about and damaging the joints. Ligaments can move slightly, but they are not stretchy like tendons.

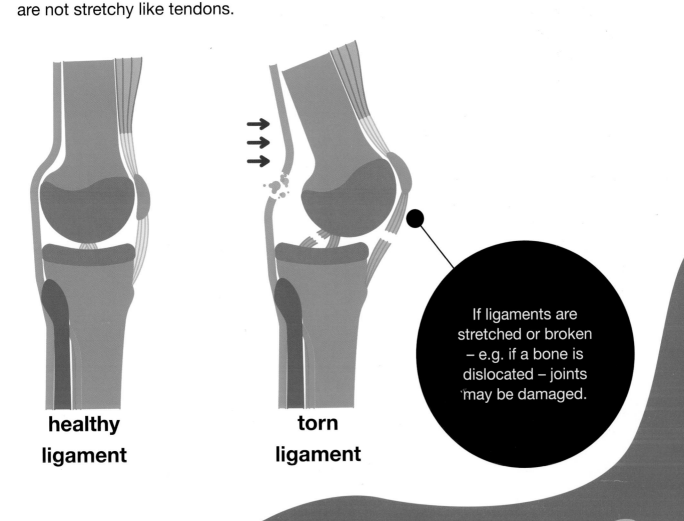

healthy ligament

torn ligament

If ligaments are stretched or broken – e.g. if a bone is dislocated – joints may be damaged.

The muscular system

The strongest muscle is the masseter – this is the muscle in your jaw that you use to chew.

Abdominal muscles help you breathe and support the spine muscles.

At just 1 mm long, your ear muscles are the shortest muscles in your body.

Your muscular system is made up of more than 650 muscles. All these muscles are connected to your bones, skin or other muscles.

Muscles lie beneath the skin, covering the bones in your skeleton. They control every movement in your body, from pushing open a door to pushing food through your digestive system.

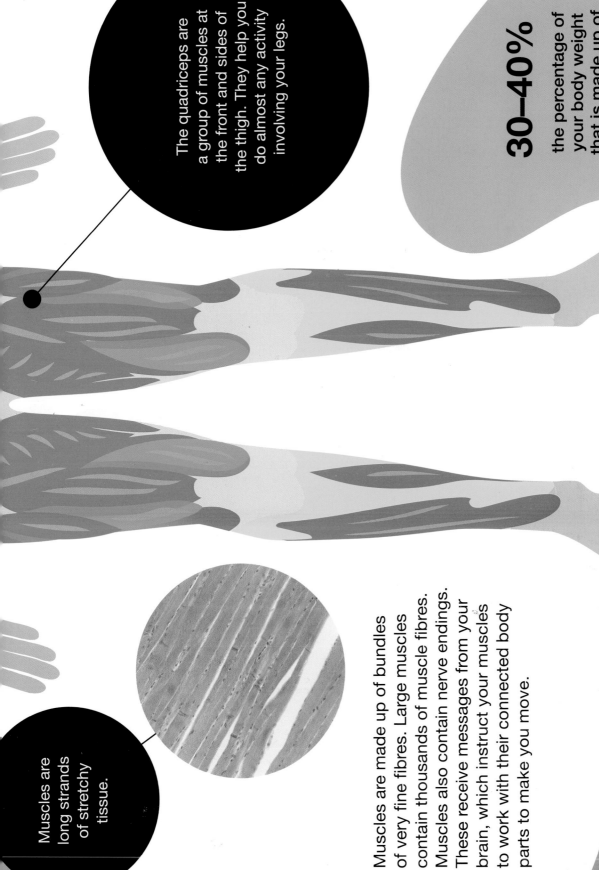

The quadriceps are a group of muscles at the front and sides of the thigh. They help you do almost any activity involving your legs.

30–40%
the percentage of your body weight that is made up of your muscles

Muscles are long strands of stretchy tissue.

Muscles are made up of bundles of very fine fibres. Large muscles contain thousands of muscle fibres. Muscles also contain nerve endings. These receive messages from your brain, which instruct your muscles to work with their connected body parts to make you move.

Types of muscle

There are three types of muscle: skeletal, smooth and cardiac. You consciously control some of these muscles, but others are involuntary – they work without any conscious instructions from you.

Cardiac muscles are a type of thick, involuntary muscle. They are only found in the wall of your heart.

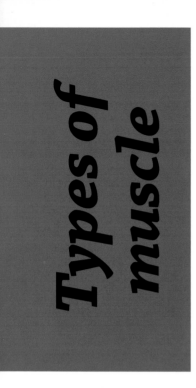

Skeletal, or voluntary, muscles are the muscles you control, such as the ones in your arms and legs (see pages 24–25). They have light and dark muscle fibres which make them look striped, or 'striated'.

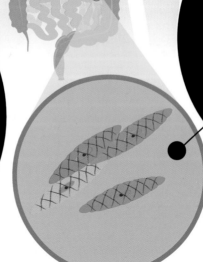

Smooth, or involuntary, muscles, like the ones in your digestive system, work without you thinking about them. They are usually in 'sheets', with one layer of muscle behind another.

Your digestive system contains a layer of smooth muscles. As these contract and relax, they help to break down food and move it through your body.

smooth muscle – relaxed

smooth muscle – contracted

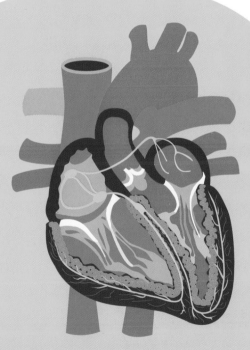

There are millions of cardiac muscle cells in your heart. They all contract at the same time, pushing blood through your heart so it can circulate through the rest of your body.

9,000 litres

the amount of blood that the muscles in your heart pump round your body in one day – that's more than 110 bathtubs of blood

Muscles and movement

Skeletal muscles work with your joints, tendons and ligaments. Together they allow you to move in many different ways.

Your brain sends instructions to your muscles through a network of nerve cells.

Movement can be as big as taking a running jump or as tiny as blinking. Even simple movements involve a lot of body parts. When you throw a ball, you are using around sixty bones, fifty joints and more than a hundred different muscles.

A muscle can only move its connected bone in one direction, so muscles work in pairs. As one muscle contracts, the other relaxes.

When the nerve cells receive these instructions, the muscles contract (get shorter). This is what makes you move.

When you flex your biceps, they contract and your triceps relax. The tendons pull on your bones, which raises your arm.

Some of the most important muscles for movement are in the arms and legs. Most of these muscles work in pairs.

biceps

triceps

biceps

triceps

To lower the arm again, the triceps contract and the biceps relax.

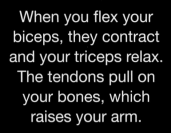

If you repeat an action over and over again, such as a tennis shot, 'muscle memory' kicks in. This is when your muscles 'learn' how to perform that action more quickly and precisely.

200

the number of muscles you use taking a single step

Facial muscles

Think of all the different emotions you show on your face: happiness, sadness, surprise, anger, fear and many more. You can make these expressions thanks to the muscles in your face.

The procerus and corrugator supercilli are just two of forty-three muscles that you use to frown.

The temporalis muscle in your temple helps you clench your teeth and chew your food.

The orbicularis oculi are the muscles near your eyes that make you blink.

The muscles responsible for facial expressions are attached to your skin, not your bones. Other facial muscles help you do things such as eat, drink, suck, blow and whistle.

The tongue is an amazing group of muscles that is attached to your body at just one end. These muscles help you chew your food and talk.

There are eight muscles in your tongue.

You use seventeen muscles to smile, including the levator labii superioris by your nose and the risorius next to your mouth.

30,000

the number of times a day the muscles that control your eyelids move as you blink – that means you spend about 10 per cent of your waking day with your eyes shut

Kissing involves thirty-four facial muscles. The most important is the orbicularis oris, which is what puckers your lips.

31

Sprains and strains

If you work your muscles really hard, they might ache or feel sore. Rest is usually enough to make them feel better, but sometimes more serious injuries can affect the ligaments, tendons and muscles.

The three lateral ligaments are the ones that are injured most easily in the ankle.

There are two other ligaments, higher up in the ankle.

A sprain is a stretch or a tear to a ligament. Most sprains happen to ankles, knees and wrists.

Small stretches or tears can make it difficult to move the bones around the joint.

Sprains and strains can cause pain, bruising, swelling and muscle spasms.

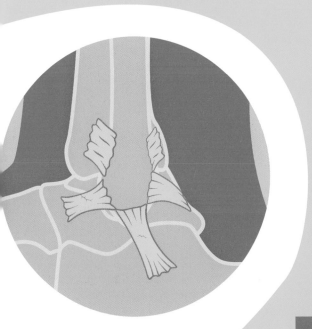

A strain is a stretch or tear to a muscle or tendon. These can happen to any part of the body, especially ones used a lot in certain sports, such as elbows or wrists in racket sports. They can make it hard to move the affected joint.

15 cm

the average length of the Achilles tendon

The Achilles tendon, from the calf to the heel, is the largest tendon in the body. This big tendon sometimes tears, making it painful and difficult to move or walk.

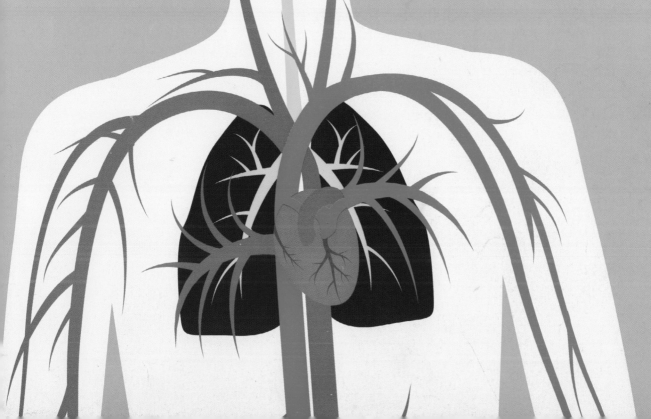

THE HEART, LUNGS AND BLOOD

Around the body

Our bodies are made up of trillions of cells. Every cell needs oxygen to produce energy. We need energy for everything that we do, so delivering oxygen to our cells is a vital process.

The respiratory system transports oxygen into the body for cells to use. The process in which cells use oxygen to produce energy is called aerobic respiration. Aerobic respiration also produces carbon dioxide. This is a waste gas that we don't need in our bodies.

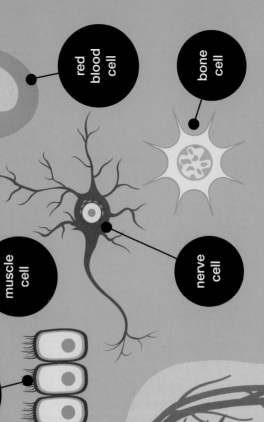

red blood cell

bone cell

muscle cell

nerve cell

intestine cell

There are many types of cells in our bodies, including nerve cells, muscle cells, intestine cells, bone cells and red blood cells (see page 54).

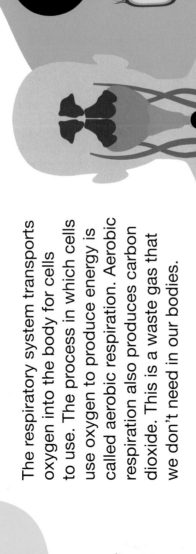

A gas exchange takes place in the lungs. Oxygen enters the blood. Carbon dioxide is removed from the blood.

Carbon dioxide leaves the body through the airways.

A network of arteries (shown in white) carries blood to the brain and across the head.

37.2 trillion

the number of cells in the human body, all of which need to be supplied with oxygen

Oxygen and carbon dioxide travel around the body through the cardiovascular system. They are carried in the blood through a network of arteries, veins and capillaries. The heart acts as a pump, moving this blood around the body to and from cells.

37

The airways

When we breathe in, air travels through the airways to the lungs. The airways include the nose, mouth, throat and trachea.

Most air enters the body through the nostrils. Mucus and tiny hairs filter the air as it travels through the nose. They trap dust and germs that could damage the lungs.

Some air enters through the mouth.

18,000– 20,000 litres

the amount of air that passes through an adult's nose every day – that's a lorry-load of air

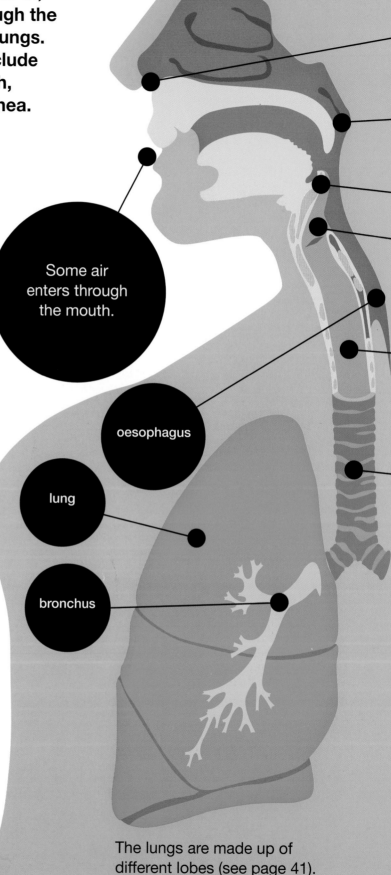

oesophagus

lung

bronchus

The lungs are made up of different lobes (see page 41).

nostrils

pharynx

Air then travels down the throat. There are two passageways in the throat – one for food (the oesophagus) and one for air (the trachea).

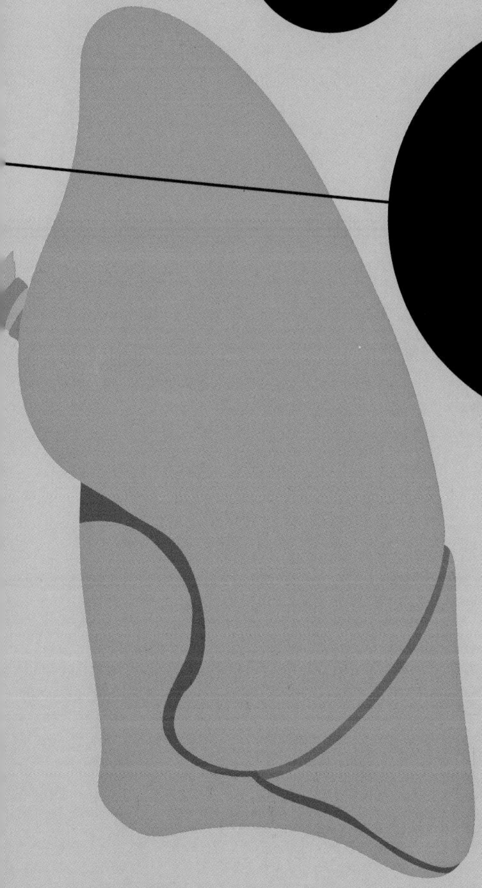

Tiny hairs called cilia cover the walls of the trachea. They trap particles that weren't caught in the nose and stop them from entering the lungs.

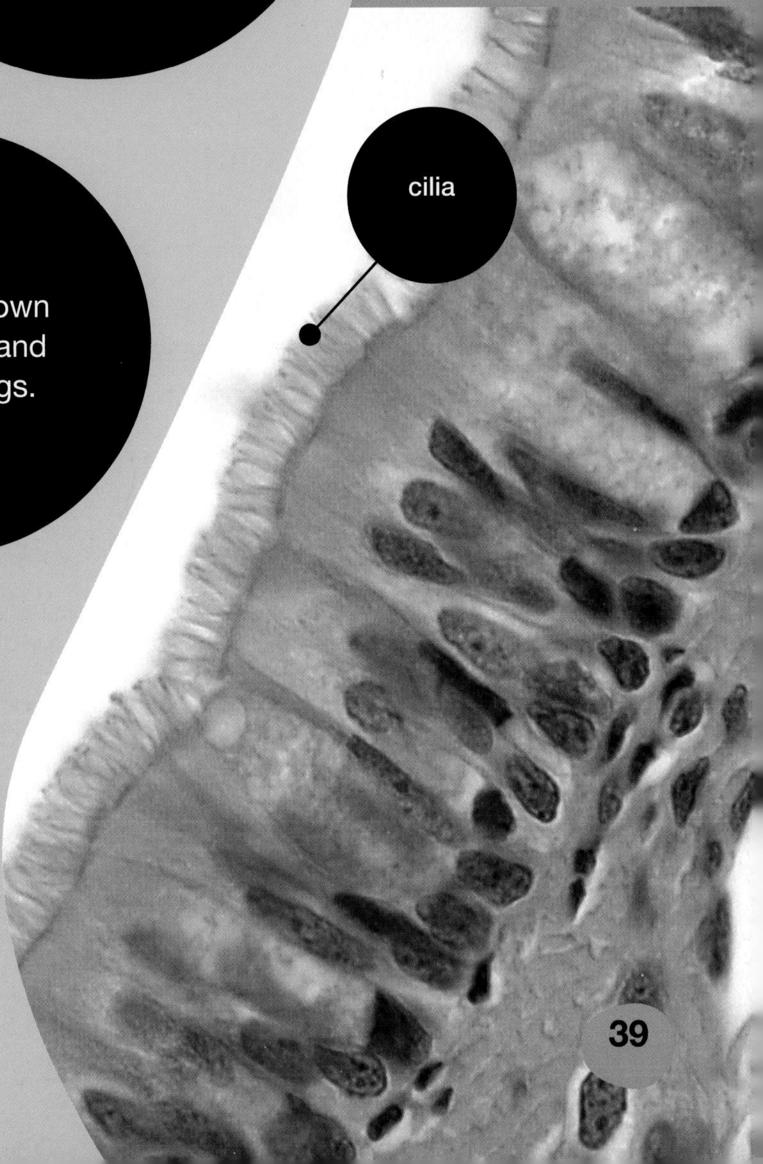

larynx

The epiglottis covers the top of the trachea. This stops food from going down into the trachea.

trachea

cilia

Air moves down the trachea and into the lungs.

The lungs are at the end of the airways and respiratory system. In the lungs, oxygen (O_2) from the air enters the blood and carbon dioxide (CO_2) is removed from the blood. This is known as gas exchange (see pages 44–45).

The bronchi are the two airways that come from the trachea into the lungs.

Bronchioles are smaller airways that come off the bronchi.

The bronchioles connect the bronchi to the alveoli. Air travels through the 1 mm-wide passageways to the alveoli, where oxygen enters the blood and carbon dioxide is removed.

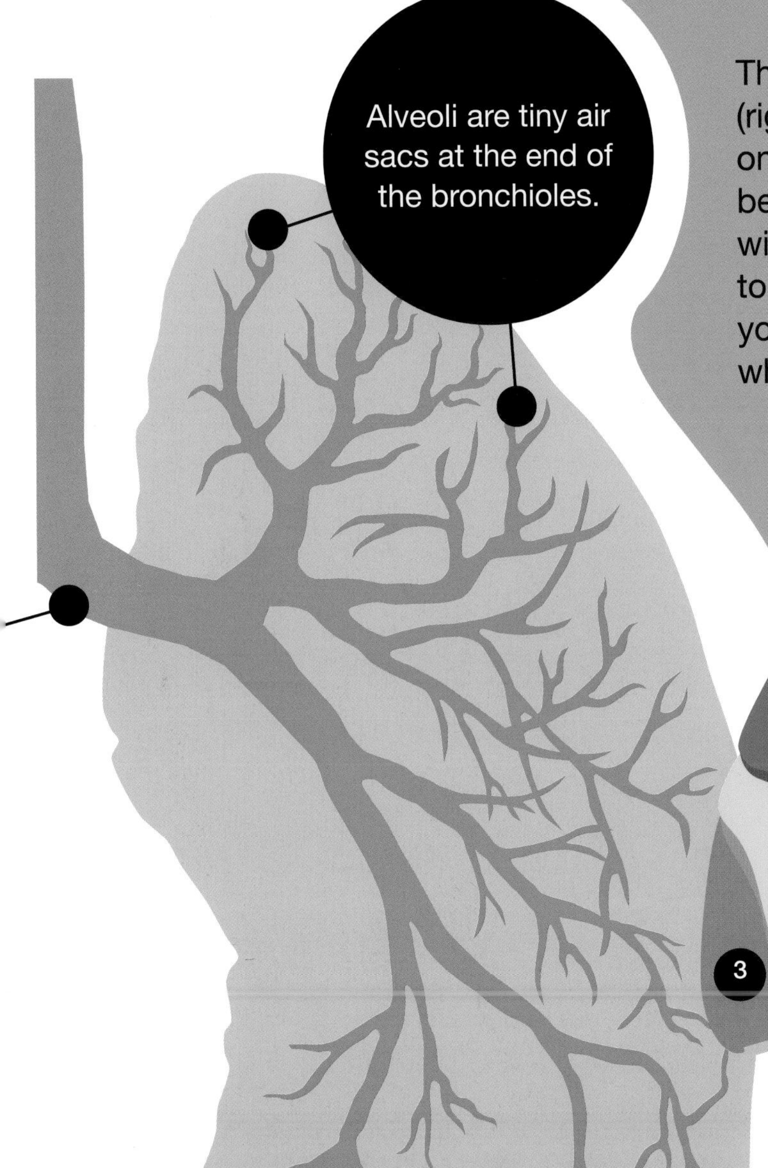

Alveoli are tiny air sacs at the end of the bronchioles.

The lung on the left side of your body (right, below) is smaller than the lung on the right side of your body (left, below) because it shares its space with the heart, which is tilted slightly to the left. The lung on the left side of your body is made up of two lobes, while your right lung has three lobes.

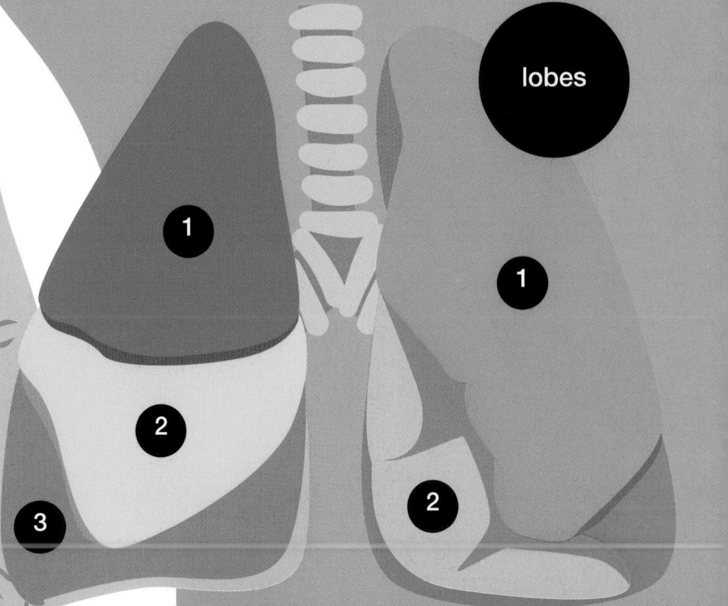

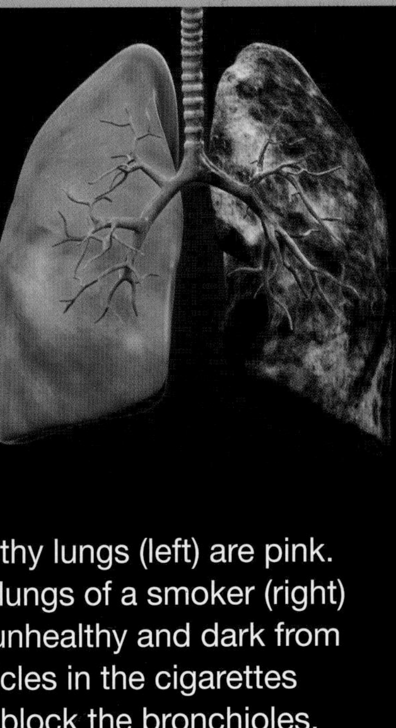

lobes

1

1

2

3

2

2,414 km

the length of the airways in the lungs

Healthy lungs (left) are pink. The lungs of a smoker (right) are unhealthy and dark from particles in the cigarettes that block the bronchioles.

41

When we inhale (breathe in) and exhale (breathe out), our ribs, lungs and diaphragm change position and shape. This movement pulls air into the body and pushes it out again.

air in

diaphragm

The diaphragm is a large, dome-shaped band of muscle between the lungs and the stomach.

The diaphragm contracts and moves down to let more air in.

inhale

During inhalation, the muscles in the ribcage and the diaphragm tighten. This makes the ribcage expand upwards and outwards to make more space. The increase in chest size creates an area of low pressure inside the body. Air is sucked into the area of low pressure, travelling through the airways and into the lungs.

As the diaphragm relaxes and the ribcage returns to its original size and position, there is less space available in the chest. As a result, air is pushed out of the body through the airways.

The lungs expand as they fill with air. They get smaller as air leaves the body.

air out

3–5 cm

the average increase in the circumference of an adult's ribcage during inhalation

exhale

43

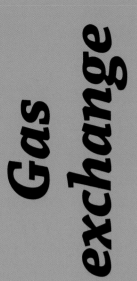

Gas exchange

Gas exchange takes place in the alveoli (see pages 40–41. Here oxygen (O_2), from the air passes into the bloodstream and carbon dioxide (CO_2) is removed.

There are around 700 million alveoli in an adult's lungs. Although they are very small, there are so many that if they were all spread out flat on the ground, they would cover a tennis court. They are surrounded by tiny blood vessels, called capillaries. The walls of the alveoli and the capillaries are so thin that gases can pass through them.

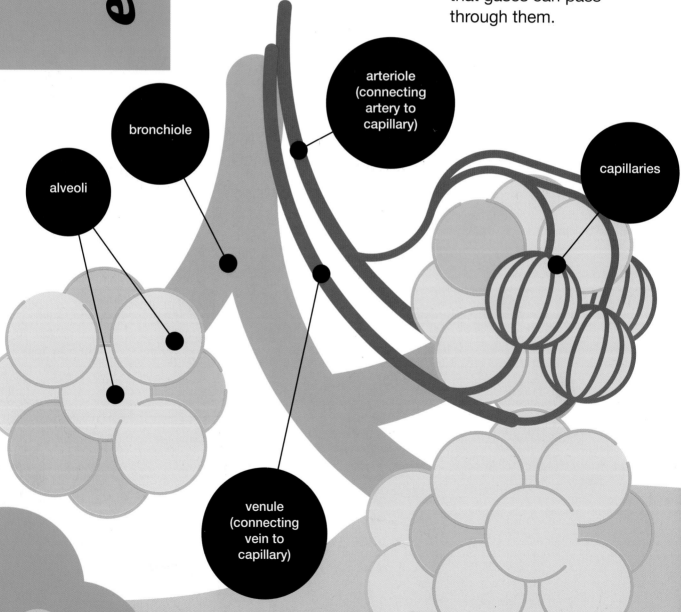

arteriole (connecting artery to capillary)

bronchiole

capillaries

alveoli

venule (connecting vein to capillary)

0.2 mm

the average diameter of an alveolus (singular of alveoli) – about the same width as a human hair

CO_2 O_2

carbon dioxide out

oxygen in

During inhalation, the alveoli fill with oxygen-rich air. Some of this oxygen passes through the walls of the alveoli into the capillary, where it is picked up by red blood cells.

Red blood cells also carry carbon dioxide, a waste gas from aerobic respiration (see pages 36–37), from cells to the lungs. This passes from the capillary into the alveoli. It leaves the body when we exhale.

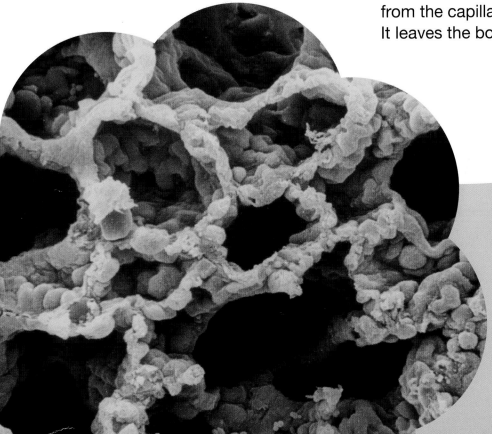

This microscopic image shows the air sacs of the alveoli and the walls where gas exchange takes place.

Sneezing and coughing

It is important for the airways to stay clear so that the body can receive oxygen. Sneezing and coughing remove particles from our airways so that we can breathe properly.

40,000
the number of saliva and mucus droplets that are released by one sneeze

Nerve endings send a signal to the brain, which triggers the sneeze or cough reflex. First, the body takes a deep breath in.

A sneeze or a cough happens when nerve endings in the nose or airways sense dust or dirt particles, pollen, or mucus.

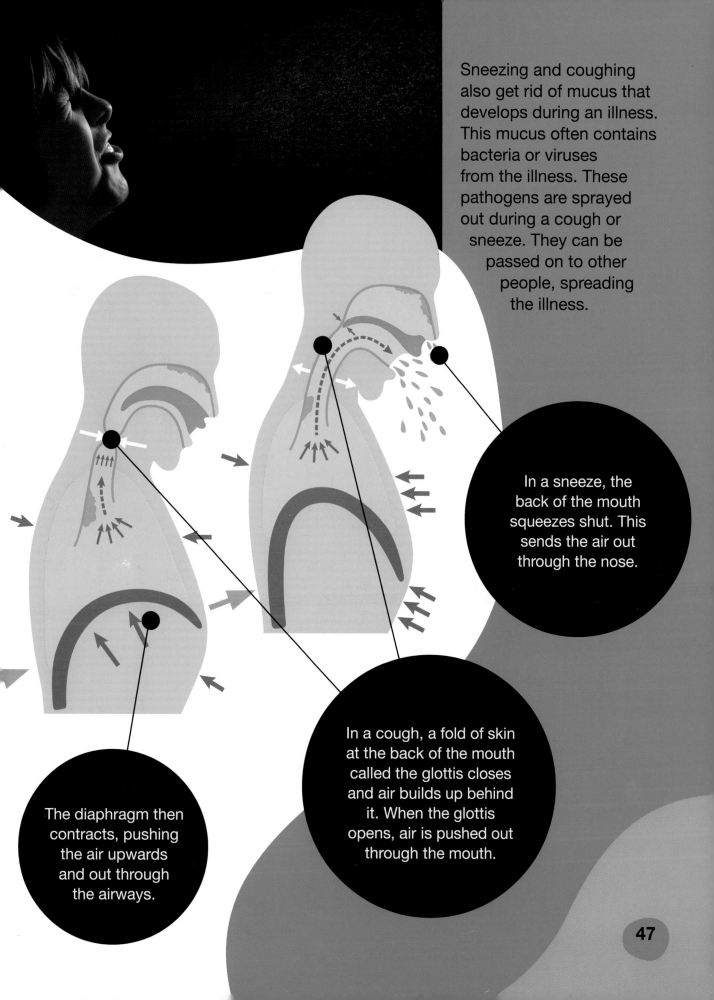

Sneezing and coughing also get rid of mucus that develops during an illness. This mucus often contains bacteria or viruses from the illness. These pathogens are sprayed out during a cough or sneeze. They can be passed on to other people, spreading the illness.

In a sneeze, the back of the mouth squeezes shut. This sends the air out through the nose.

In a cough, a fold of skin at the back of the mouth called the glottis closes and air builds up behind it. When the glottis opens, air is pushed out through the mouth.

The diaphragm then contracts, pushing the air upwards and out through the airways.

Respiratory illnesses

The respiratory system is often affected by illnesses. These range from mild diseases, such as the common cold, to serious conditions, such as asthma and pneumonia.

Infections are common in the respiratory system. Bacteria and viruses are breathed in through the nose and mouth and can affect areas along the airways. The most common respiratory disease is the cold, which affects the nose and the throat. Pneumonia is a serious infection of the lungs.

During pneumonia, the alveoli in the lungs become inflamed and fill with pus and mucus.

Patients with pneumonia cough to get rid of the mucus and pus through the airways.

Other symptoms of pneumonia include fever, difficulty breathing and chest pain.

healthy

pneumonia

fluid in alveolus

alveolus

Asthma is an inflammation of the airways and lungs. The airways become smaller, which makes it harder to breathe. During an asthma attack, the airways can close almost entirely. Some people are born with asthma, while some people develop it because of air pollution or an allergy to pollen.

Some people with asthma have more mucus than normal. They cough to get rid of it.

The airways of people with asthma are always narrow, but they become even narrower during an asthma attack.

 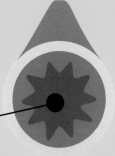 

normal **asthma** **asthma attack**

7–10%

the percentage of children that have asthma

Inhalers filled with medicine help to lessen the symptoms of asthma by reducing inflammation and widening the airways.

49

The heart

The heart is a powerful muscle that pumps oxygenated blood around the body, on its way to cells. It is positioned between the lungs, tilted slightly to the left of the body.

The heart is divided into left and right sides. Each side has two chambers. The top chambers are called atria and the bottom chambers are called ventricles.

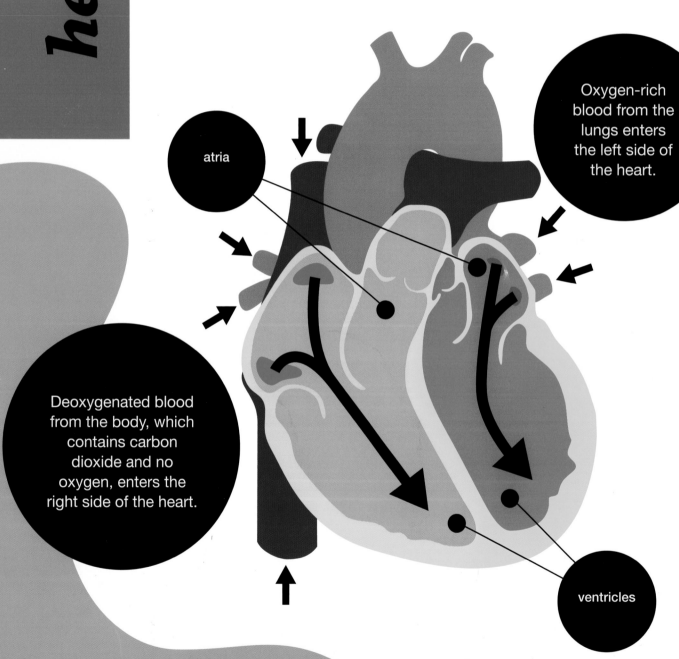

atria

Oxygen-rich blood from the lungs enters the left side of the heart.

Deoxygenated blood from the body, which contains carbon dioxide and no oxygen, enters the right side of the heart.

ventricles

The oxygen-rich blood goes from the heart to the rest of the body.

7,500 litres

the quantity of blood pumped by an adult heart every day – the equivalent of over 20 bathtubs

The deoxygenated blood is pumped back to the lungs, so that it can become oxygenated through gas exchange.

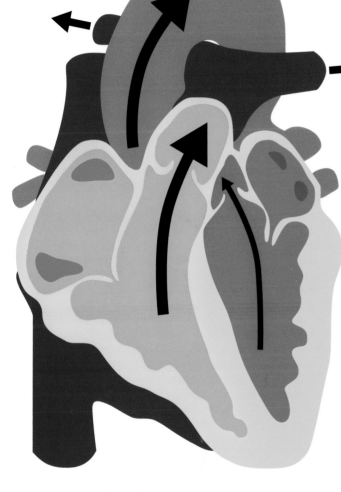

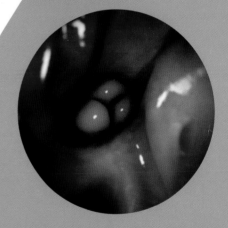

Natural electrical impulses make the heart muscles contract and relax. First, the atria contract, pushing blood into the ventricles. Then, the ventricles contract, pushing blood out of the heart.

This is a pulmonary valve – one of four valves in the heart. Valves open to let blood flow through and then close to stop it from flowing backwards. The sound of a heartbeat is actually the sound of a valve closing.

A healthy heart

It is important to keep the heart healthy and working well. Doing exercise and eating a balanced diet help to prevent problems such as heart disease and heart attacks.

This is the artery of someone suffering from heart disease. The purple area is the fatty material blocking the artery.

Heart disease is a build up of fatty material in the coronary arteries – the arteries that supply blood to the heart. The arteries become narrow, which makes it hard for the heart to receive enough oxygen-rich blood. This is painful, uncomfortable and dangerous.

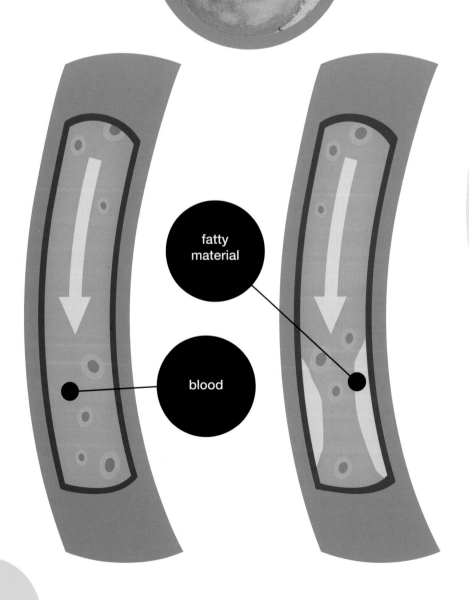

fatty material

blood

If a piece of the fatty material breaks off, it can form a blood clot. A blood clot can block a coronary artery, stopping oxygen from reaching the heart. Without oxygen, the heart muscles begin to die. This is known as a heart attack. Heart attacks can be fatal.

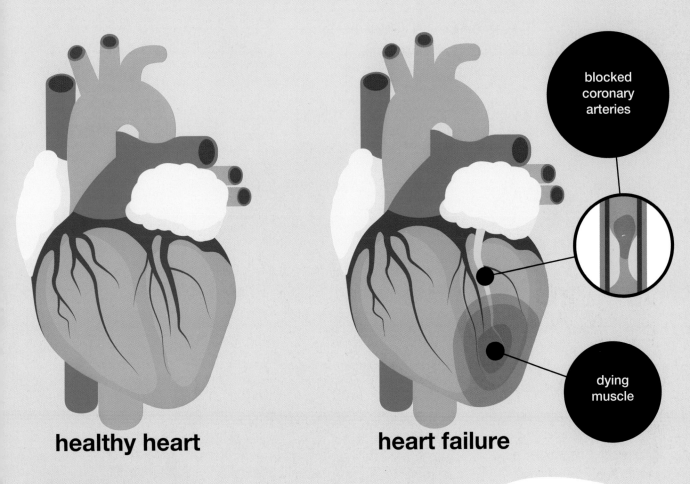

healthy heart

heart failure

blocked coronary arteries

dying muscle

24%

the increased risk of developing heart disease of a smoker compared to a non-smoker

Eating a healthy, balanced diet and doing regular exercise are the best ways to keep the heart healthy. Eating too much salt, smoking and obesity increase the risk of developing heart disease. Most people affected by heart disease and heart attacks are adults, but it is important for young people to develop good health habits.

Blood

Blood is made up of red blood cells, white blood cells, platelets and plasma. It transports materials around the body, and it is also involved in the body's immune system (see pages 60–61).

5 litres

the amount of blood in the average adult's body, around 7 per cent of the total body weight

Plasma is one of the main ingredients in blood. It is a liquid, mainly made up of water. Plasma carries nutrients, hormones and waste around the body. Red blood cells are the other main component. As we've seen, they transport oxygen to cells around the body. Platelets help blood to clot, while white blood cells are part of the immune system.

blood structure

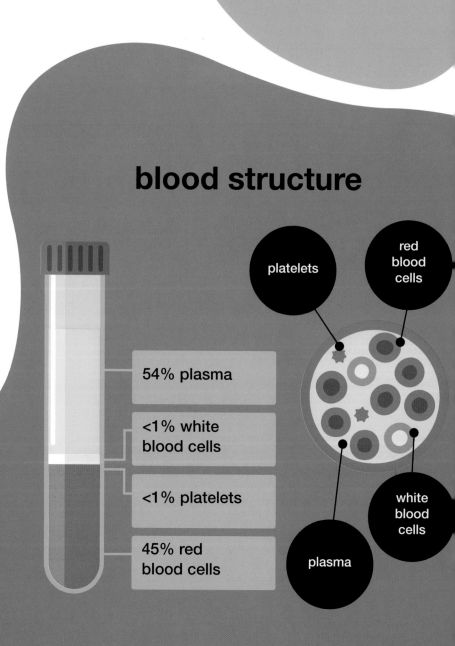

54% plasma

<1% white blood cells

<1% platelets

45% red blood cells

platelets

red blood cells

plasma

white blood cells

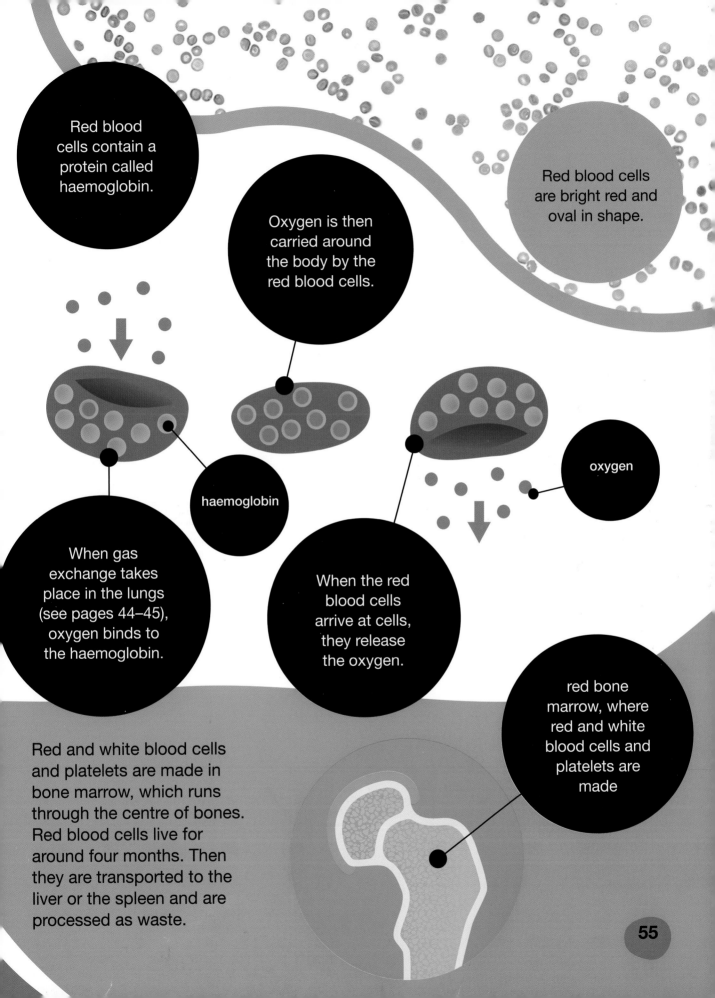

Red blood cells contain a protein called haemoglobin.

Oxygen is then carried around the body by the red blood cells.

Red blood cells are bright red and oval in shape.

haemoglobin

oxygen

When gas exchange takes place in the lungs (see pages 44–45), oxygen binds to the haemoglobin.

When the red blood cells arrive at cells, they release the oxygen.

red bone marrow, where red and white blood cells and platelets are made

Red and white blood cells and platelets are made in bone marrow, which runs through the centre of bones. Red blood cells live for around four months. Then they are transported to the liver or the spleen and are processed as waste.

Blood vessels

100,000 km

the combined length of blood vessels in the human body – enough to go around the world two and a half times

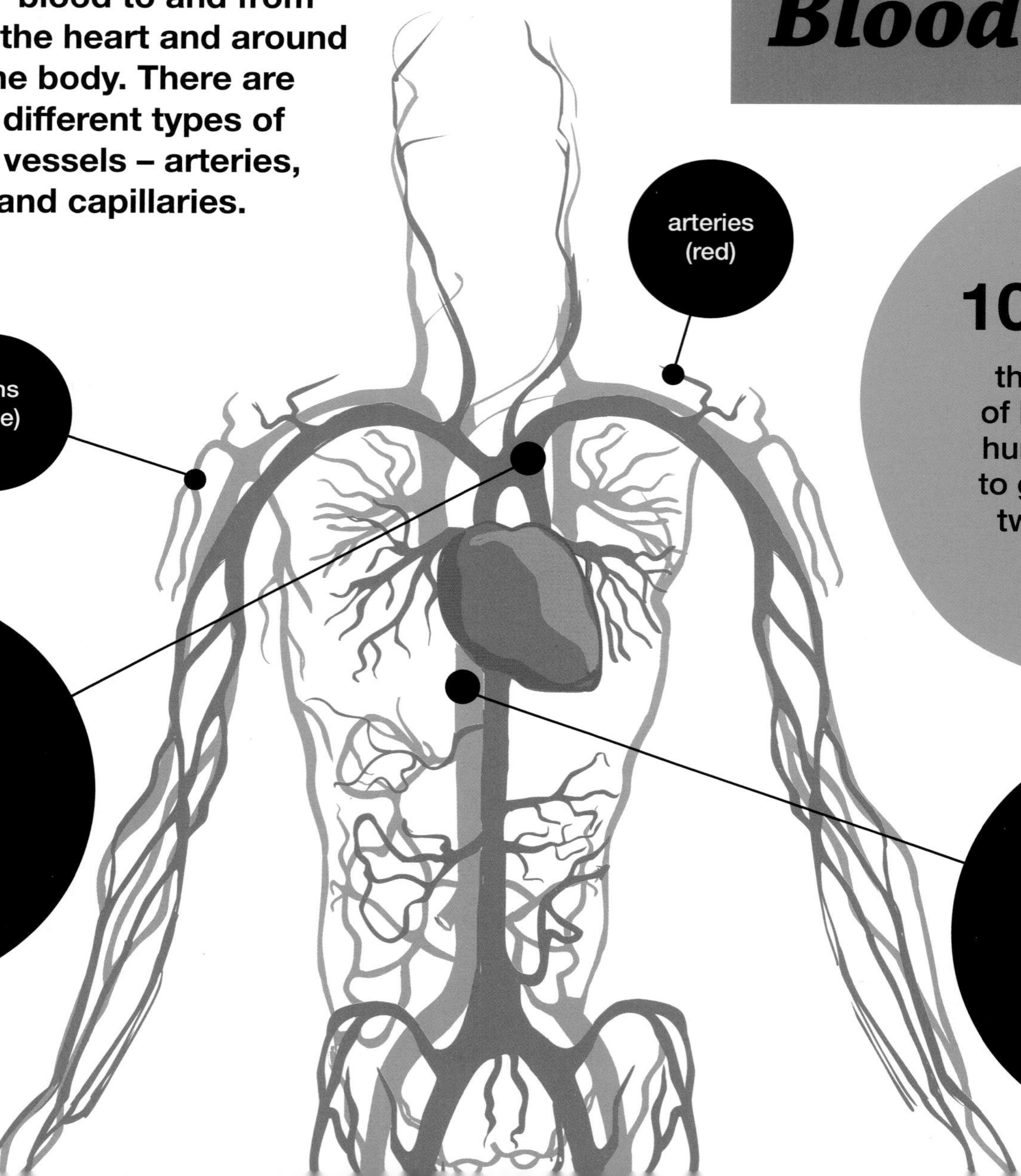

The vena cava is the body's largest vein. It leads back to the heart and returns blood from the entire body.

arteries (red)

Blood vessels carry blood to and from the heart and around the body. There are three different types of blood vessels – arteries, veins and capillaries.

veins (blue)

The aorta is the largest artery in the body. It comes directly out of the heart.

56

Capillaries are the tiny blood vessels that go to individual cells and tissue. They split apart and join back together, forming a web. The walls of capillaries are so thin that oxygen, nutrients and water can pass through the wall and into the cell. Carbon dioxide passes the other way and enters the bloodstream in the capillary.

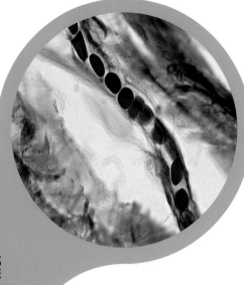

Most capillaries are so narrow that red blood cells can only pass through in single file.

Arteries carry oxygen-rich blood from the heart to cells around the body. The blood inside arteries is at high pressure, so arteries have thick walls to withstand this. Veins carry blood back to the heart. The blood in veins is at a lower pressure, so they have thinner walls.

vein

There are valves in veins to stop blood flowing in the wrong direction. Every time the heart beats, valves open to let blood through. The valves then close to stop the blood flowing backwards.

artery

Arteries do not need valves because the pressure from the heart is so strong that blood is only able to flow in one direction.

Blood groups

There are four different types of blood – A, B, AB and O. Each type of blood can also be positive (+) or negative (-), for example B+ or O-. Each blood group has slightly different red blood cells and antibodies.

Blood groups are very important when it comes to blood transfusions. If someone loses a lot of blood in an accident or through illness, they might need an injection of blood taken from another person's body.

Blood transfusions have to be from the correct blood group (see chart to the right). Some groups of blood can be given to people from other groups and some can't. It can make people very sick if they receive the wrong type of blood.

Blood from *positive*-type donors can only be given to people with compatible *positive* blood. Blood from *negative*-type donors can be given to compatible *positive* and *negative* recipients.

blood-type compatibility chart

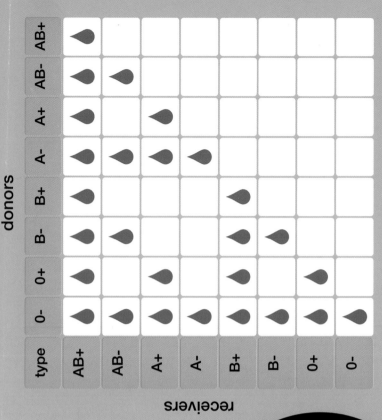

donors

type	O-	O+	B-	B+	A-	A+	AB-	AB+
AB+	●	●	●	●	●	●	●	●
AB-	●		●		●		●	
A+	●	●			●	●		
A-	●				●			
B+	●	●	●	●				
B-	●		●					
O+	●	●						
O-	●							

receivers

If both parents have a negative blood group, their child will also be negative. Otherwise, their child could be positive or negative.

Blood is tested in hospitals so that the blood group can be identified.

Blood groups are passed down from parents to children. Each person has two blood group genes. One comes from each parent.

A and B blood group genes are dominant. This means if someone has one of these genes, this will be their blood group.

A and B blood group genes can combine. If someone has one of each, their blood group is AB.

blood type B

blood type A

blood type
O

blood type
B

blood type
AB

blood type
A

- blood type **A**
- blood type **B**
- blood type **O**

O blood group genes are recessive. This means a person will only have this blood group if both of their blood group genes are O.

59

The immune system

The body's immune system protects it from pathogens, such as bacteria, that can cause disease. Blood plays an important role in the immune system, helping to close wounds and fighting dangerous pathogens.

When we cut ourselves, platelets in the blood clump together at the wound. They plug the hole to stop blood from leaving the body and to stop pathogens from entering the body.

Platelets and red blood cells gather around the wound.

Platelets release a chemical that makes plasma turn into a stringy substance called fibrin.

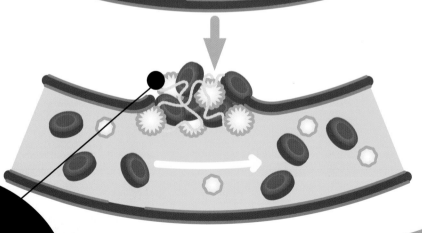

The fibrin forms a mesh across the wound, which traps the platelets and blood cells. This dries into a scab, closing the wound.

Red blood cells and platelets (pink) trapped in a fibrin net can be seen through a microscope.

When pathogens get inside the body, different types of white blood cells help to destroy them. Some white blood cells surround and ingest pathogens. Others produce antibodies that stick on to pathogens and stop them from damaging the body.

150,000–400,000 per cubic mm

the average number of platelets in blood

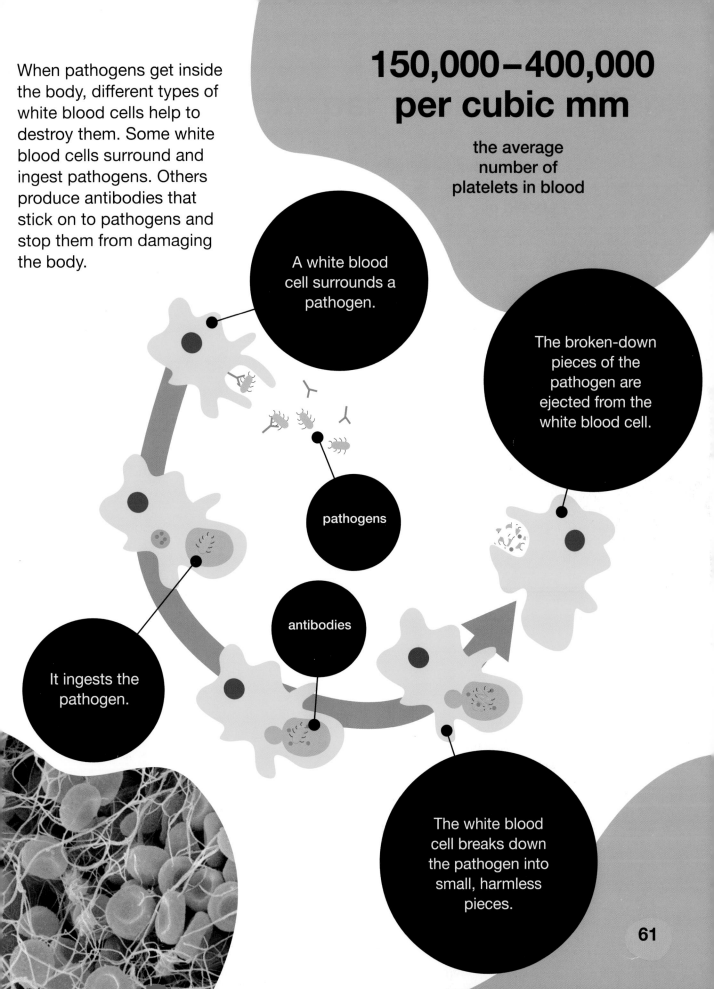

A white blood cell surrounds a pathogen.

The broken-down pieces of the pathogen are ejected from the white blood cell.

pathogens

antibodies

It ingests the pathogen.

The white blood cell breaks down the pathogen into small, harmless pieces.

61

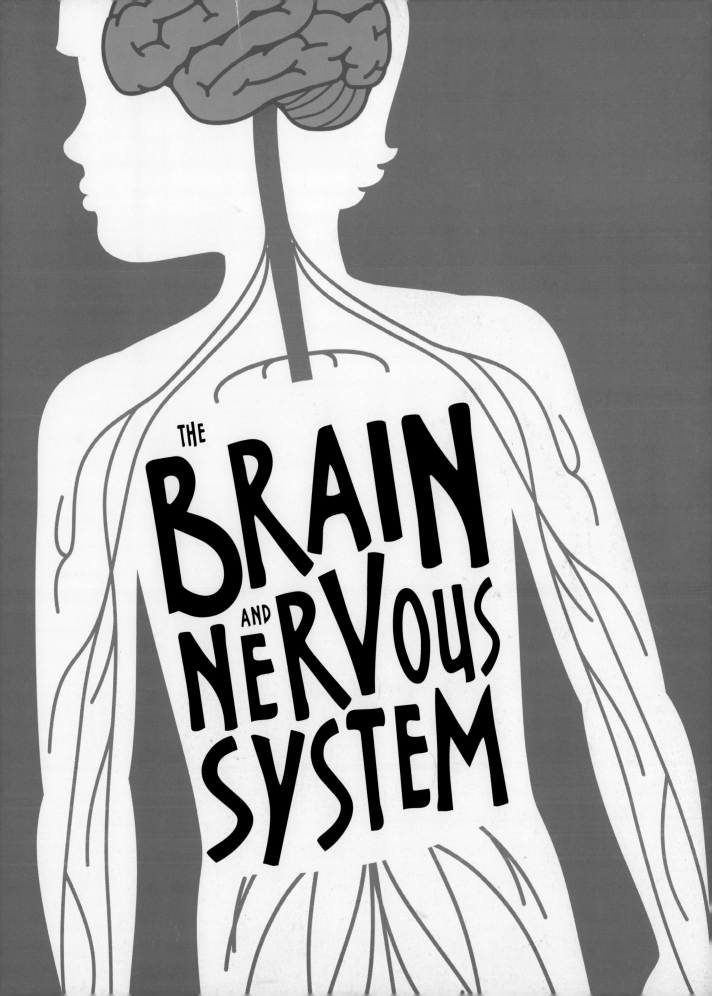

THE BRAIN AND NERVOUS SYSTEM

The *nervous system*

The nervous system is the body's main communication network. Information and instructions travel through the nervous system as electrical signals.

The nervous system is made up of two main parts – the central nervous system and the peripheral nervous system. The peripheral nervous system transports information from sensory organs, such as the eyes, to the central nervous system. It also carries instructions from the central nervous system (the brain and spinal cord) back to the rest of the body.

The central nervous system is made up of the brain and spinal cord.

The peripheral nervous system is made up of nerves – long bundles of **neurones** (nerve cells, see pages 68–69).

64

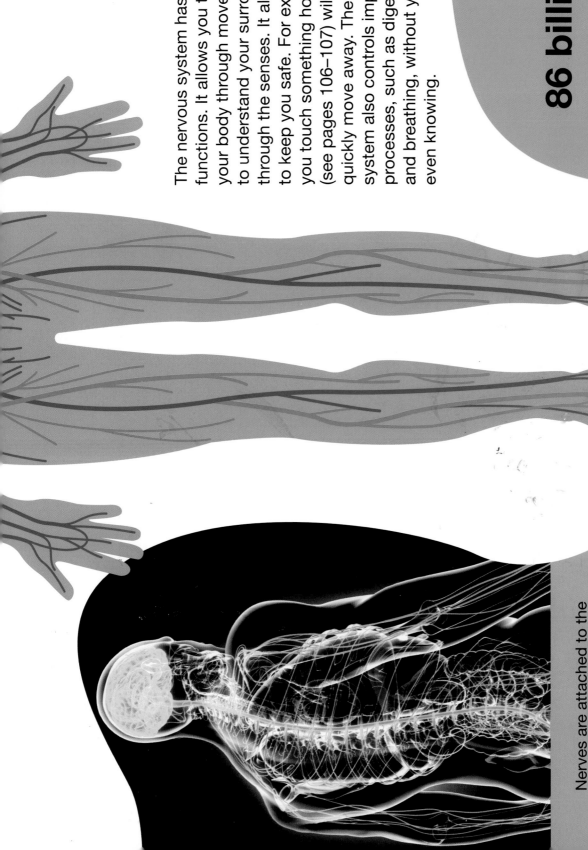

The nervous system has many functions. It allows you to control your body through movement and to understand your surroundings through the senses. It also helps to keep you safe. For example, if you touch something hot, a reflex (see pages 106–107) will make you quickly move away. The nervous system also controls important processes, such as digestion and breathing, without you even knowing.

86 billion
the number of neurones in the brain

Nerves are attached to the brain and the spinal cord.

The brain

The brain is the body's control centre. It interprets signals from receptors (cells that receive sensory information) and sends out messages to effectors (such as muscles and glands). It also controls other important functions, allowing you to think, plan, remember and imagine.

20%
the amount of the body's oxygen and blood used by the brain when awake

The temporal lobe is in charge of speech, hearing and memories.

The brain has three main parts: the cerebrum, the cerebellum and the brainstem. The cerebrum is the top, outer layer of the brain. It controls speech, thought and high-level intelligence.

The folded surface of the cerebrum can be seen in this real human brain, preserved in chemicals to stop it from decaying.

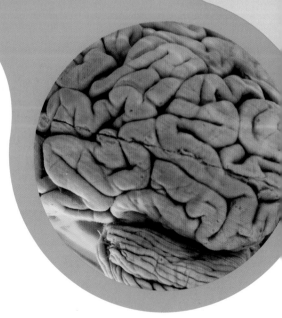

The cerebrum is divided into halves, called hemispheres.

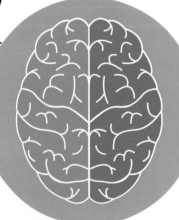

Each half of the cerebrum can be divided into four major regions, called lobes. Each lobe carries out a different function. Most actions controlled by the brain rely on activity from a combination of different lobes.

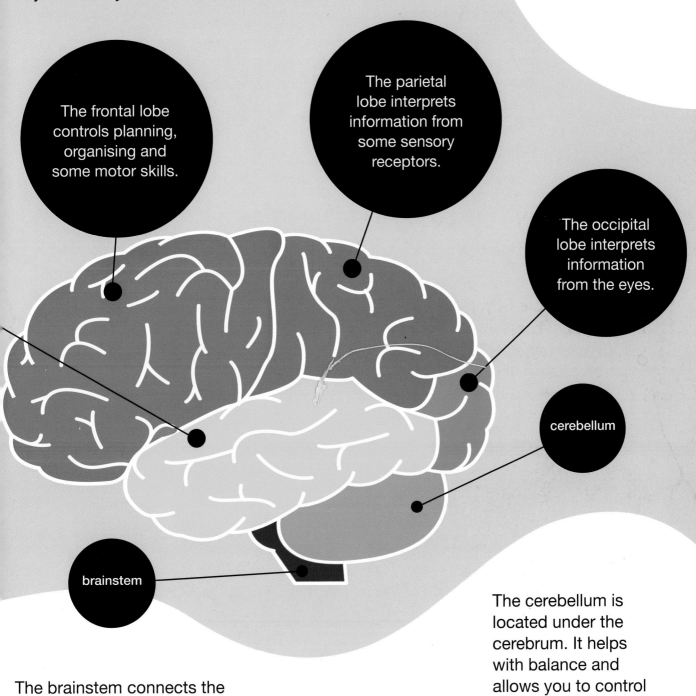

The frontal lobe controls planning, organising and some motor skills.

The parietal lobe interprets information from some sensory receptors.

The occipital lobe interprets information from the eyes.

cerebellum

brainstem

The cerebellum is located under the cerebrum. It helps with balance and allows you to control your movements.

The brainstem connects the cerebrum to the spinal cord. It controls unconscious activities, such as your breathing and heartbeat (see pages 82–83).

Neurones

Neurones are nerve cells. They connect to each other to create a network around the body. Electrical signals travel around this network, carrying messages throughout the nervous system.

There are three different types of nerve cell:

- Sensory neurones carry signals from receptors to the central nervous system.
- Relay neurones carry signals within the central nervous system.
- Motor neurones carry signals from the central nervous system to effectors.

types of neurone

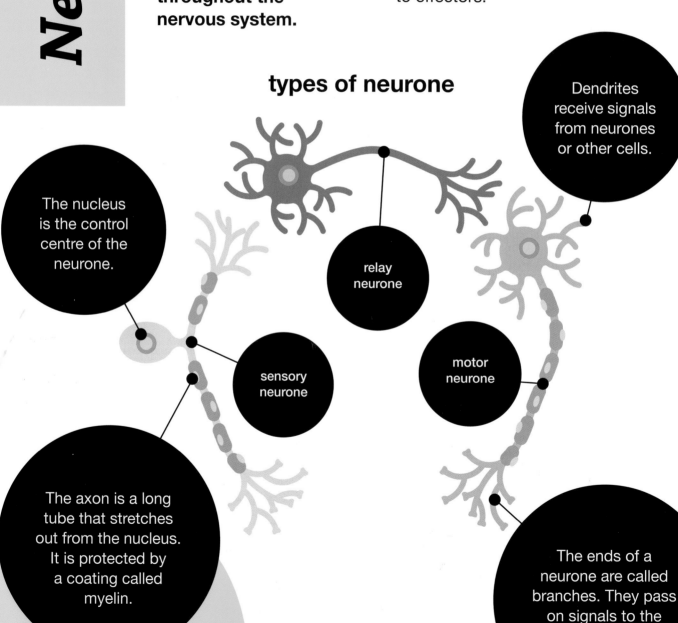

Dendrites receive signals from neurones or other cells.

The nucleus is the control centre of the neurone.

relay neurone

sensory neurone

motor neurone

The axon is a long tube that stretches out from the nucleus. It is protected by a coating called myelin.

The ends of a neurone are called branches. They pass on signals to the dendrites of other neurones.

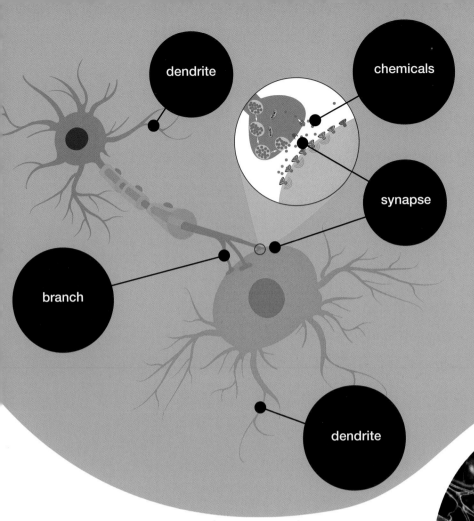

dendrite

chemicals

synapse

branch

dendrite

Neurones are separated from each other by a microscopic gap called a synapse. When a signal reaches the end of a branch, the neurones send chemicals across this gap. The dendrites of the next neurone sense the chemicals and send on the signal as an electrical impulse.

When you learn a new skill, such as riding a bike, it can trigger the creation of new synapses. This is partly why you improve at the skill over time. Synapses can also be lost over time if a skill is not practised.

120 m/s

the speed at which some electrical signals travel around the nervous system, which is four times as fast as a cheetah at top speed

Some neurones are connected to thousands of other neurones.

Nerves

Nerves are long bundles of axons that extend from nerve cells. Most nerves connect to the spinal cord, but some connect to the brain. The ends of axons can join on to muscle (to allow movement) or sensory receptors (to receive sensory information).

Each nerve is made up of bundles of axons, called fascicles. There are several fascicles in every nerve. Nerves also contain blood vessels, which bring oxygen and nutrients to cells, and carry away carbon dioxide and other waste products. The fascicles and blood vessels are contained within myelin, which prevents damage to the nerve.

cross-section of a nerve

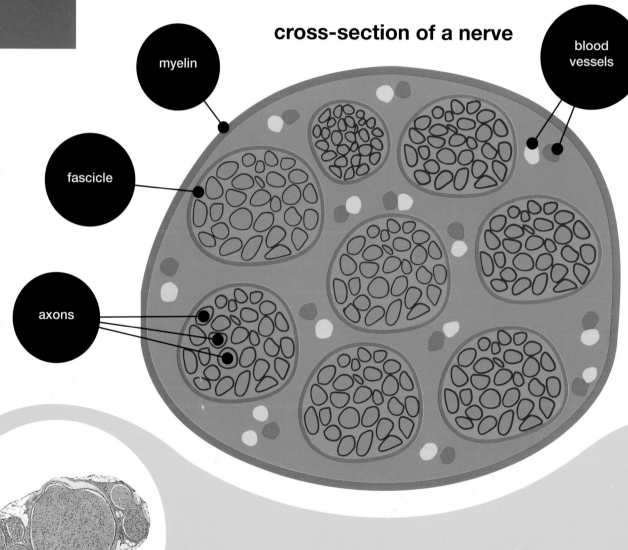

myelin

blood vessels

fascicle

axons

The fascicles in a nerve are often different sizes, as shown in this cross-section of a nerve.

1 mm

the width of the largest-known axon, found in the giant squid – it's 1,000 times the diameter of those found in the human body

Cranial nerves connect the brain with other parts of the head, face and neck. There are twelve pairs of cranial nerves, including the optic nerves, the facial nerves and the olfactory nerves.

The optic nerves carry visual information from the eyes to the brain.

The olfactory nerves send messages about smells to the brain.

The oculomotor nerves control movement of the eyes and the eyelid.

The trigeminal nerves are responsible for biting and chewing.

The vestibulocochlear nerves carry sound information from the ears to the brain.

The facial nerves help to create facial expressions.

The spinal cord and nerves

The spinal cord connects the brain to the body. It stretches from the brainstem to the lower back. Spinal nerves come off the spinal cord and extend into the arms, legs and abdomen.

The spinal cord contains billions of neurones. These neurones are protected by three layers of tissue, called meninges. The space underneath the middle meninx (singular of meninges) is filled with fluid. Vertebrae (the bones that make up the spine) surround the spinal cord.

meninges (protective layers)

spinal cord

vertebra

spinal nerves

Over thirty pairs of spinal nerves are connected to the spinal cord. Some are sensory nerves, connecting to sensory receptors, while others are motor nerves that stimulate muscles. The nerves are at their largest close to the spinal cord. They become narrower and split into thinner branches as they extend out into the body.

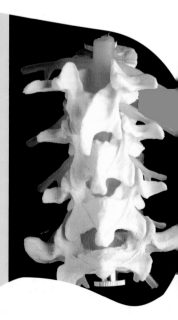

This model of the vertebrae and spinal cord shows how the spinal nerves (in orange) extend through gaps between the bones.

spinal nerves

The median nerves control the front of the forearm and parts of the hand.

The thoracic nerves control muscles in the back and the neck.

The radial nerves control the back of the arms and the wrists.

The lumbar nerves extend out into the back.

The sciatic nerves are connected to most of the skin on the legs and the muscles on the back of the thigh and foot.

The sacral nerves control much of the hips, thighs and legs, and are connected to internal organs, such as the large intestine and bladder.

1 m
the length of the longest nerve in the human body, the sciatic nerve, which stretches from the spinal cord to the toes

Receptors

Receptors are specialised cells that sense changes in the environment. They inform the brain of this new information via signals sent along nerves.

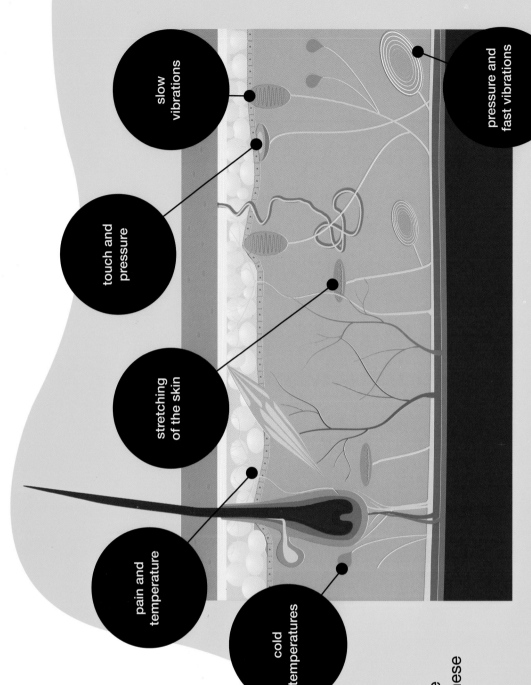

slow vibrations

touch and pressure

pressure and fast vibrations

stretching of the skin

pain and temperature

cold temperatures

Receptors are often found in sensory organs, such as the skin, mouth and nose. Different receptors are sensitive to different stimuli, including temperature, pressure, light, sound, changes in movement and position, chemicals, and pain.

touch

There are several types of receptors in the skin, which are sensitive to different stimuli. These receptors give us information about things that we touch.

Microvilli at the top of the taste receptor cells detect molecules in food.

The taste receptor cells send a signal to the brain to inform it of the molecules detected.

Signals from the taste receptor cells travel to the brain along nerves.

taste

Taste receptor cells are found in taste buds on the tongue, cheek and upper oesophagus (the tube that connects the mouth to the stomach). They recognise molecules from any substance that enters the mouth and send signals to the brain. The brain interprets the molecules as different flavours.

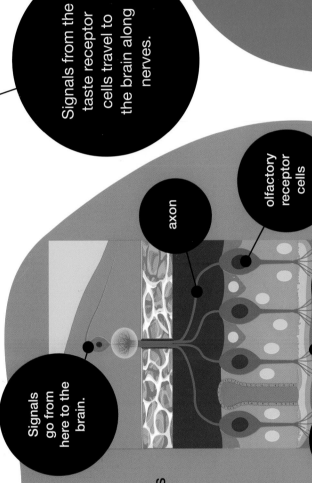

axon

olfactory receptor cells

tiny hairs

air

Signals go from here to the brain.

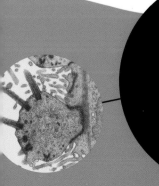

The tiny hairs on an olfactory receptor cell can be seen when viewed through a microscope.

smell

Olfactory receptors are responsible for your sense of smell. They are located behind the nose on the roof of the nasal cavity. Tiny hairs on olfactory receptor cells pick up odour molecules from any substance that enters the nose and send this information to the brain. The brain interprets this information as smell.

Seeing and hearing

Specialised receptor cells in the eyes and the ears allow us to see and hear. The information from these cells is interpreted by the brain, helping us to make sense of the objects and sounds around us.

The retina is found at the back of the eye. It contains photoreceptor cells called rods and cones that are sensitive to different colours and strengths of light. When light hits the photoreceptor cells, the cells convert it into electrical signals, which travel to the brain along the optic nerves.

retina (shown in red)

Cones are sensitive to bright and coloured light.

optic nerve

Rods are sensitive to dim light and black and white colours. They are responsible for night vision.

8.3%

the percentage of men who are affected by red-green colour blindness – the inability to differentiate between red and green. It is caused by a cone fault. Only 0.5 per cent of women are affected.

Sounds travel through the air in waves. They travel inside the ear and make the eardrum (a thin membrane) vibrate. These vibrations are passed on through the ear until they reach the cochlea, deep in the inner ear.

eardrum

tiny bones

The vestibular nerve uses hair cells to sense changes in the position and movement of the body.

cochlea

cochlear nerve

Hair cells in one section of the cochlea pick up vibrations. These cells turn the vibrations into electrical signals and send these messages to the brain along the cochlear nerves. The brain interprets this information into the sounds that we hear.

hair cells

membrane

cochlear nerve

Cochlear implants are devices that convert sounds to electrical signals. They send the signals straight to the brain, bypassing the ears. They allow some people with hearing loss to hear.

Motor neurones carry signals to effectors – parts of the body that produce a response. Effectors can be muscles, such as those in the arms, or glands, such as the pancreas.

Messages from the central nervous system are transmitted to muscles along nerves. The messages instruct muscles to contract or relax. Some muscles pull on bones that move the body's joints and limbs. Other muscles in internal organs help with tasks, such as breathing and swallowing.

Neurones connect to the membranes that cover muscles.

Nerves, muscles and bones work together to control movement.

The brain sends signals to glands to make them release hormones that control important processes in the body. Glands respond to nerve signals more slowly than muscles, releasing hormones gradually over a longer period of time.

The pineal gland releases melatonin, which helps to control the body's sleep schedule.

The pituitary gland releases hormones that control growth, blood pressure and temperature control.

The thyroid releases hormones that control how much energy the body uses.

In a female system, the ovaries release oestrogen, which controls the menstrual cycle.

The pancreas releases hormones that controls the amount of sugar in the blood.

The adrenal glands release adrenaline, which is important in the fight or flight response (see pages 80–81).

1 cm

the average diameter of the pituitary gland, which is around the same size as a pea

79

The limbic system

The limbic system is a set of structures underneath the cerebrum in the brain. Some parts of the limbic system control memory, while others deal with emotional responses, which can trigger reactions, such as the fight or flight response.

The thalamus receives signals from sensory organs and sends them on to other parts of the brain.

The hypothalamus controls body temperature and hunger.

The pituitary gland controls and releases hormones.

The amygdala is responsible for emotional responses.

The hippocampus deals with memories (see pages 84–85).

When something good happens, the amygdala creates feelings of happiness and joy. When something bad or scary happens, the amygdala creates feelings of fear and sadness. It is likely emotions would have benefited early humans, as they prepare you for behaving in a particular way. For instance, fear can trigger the fight or flight response.

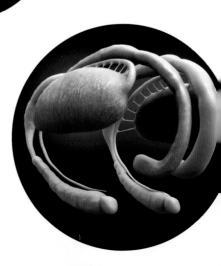

The fight or flight response is a very fast physical reaction to a potential threat. When you face a danger, messages travel from your limbic system to your body, warning you to 'be afraid', and unconsciously preparing your body to fight against the danger or to run away. As a result, your heart rate increases and your airways relax so that more blood is pumped around the body. This provides more energy to cells. Muscles tense and you become more alert.

20–60 minutes

the amount of time it takes for the body to return to normal after the fight or flight response has been triggered

Nerves carry visual information about the threat to the occipital lobe.

The occipital lobe recognises the threat and sends the information to the amygdala.

The amygdala starts the fight or flight response, in connection with the hypothalamus.

This computer-generated image shows the two parts of the limbic system – one on each side of the brain.

Signals to start the fight or flight response travel across the body via nerves.

Effectors around the body carry out the fight or flight response.

81

Unconscious actions

The nervous system controls many unconscious actions, such as digestion and heart rate. Most of the time, you aren't aware of these processes and don't control them.

Letting unconscious actions happen automatically frees up space for the brain to focus on more important and complicated tasks. Having to remember to breathe, blink or digest food would be very difficult and would take up a lot of time. While you can deliberately carry out some unconscious actions, such as breathing and blinking, most of the time you will eventually stop focusing on these actions and they will become unconscious again.

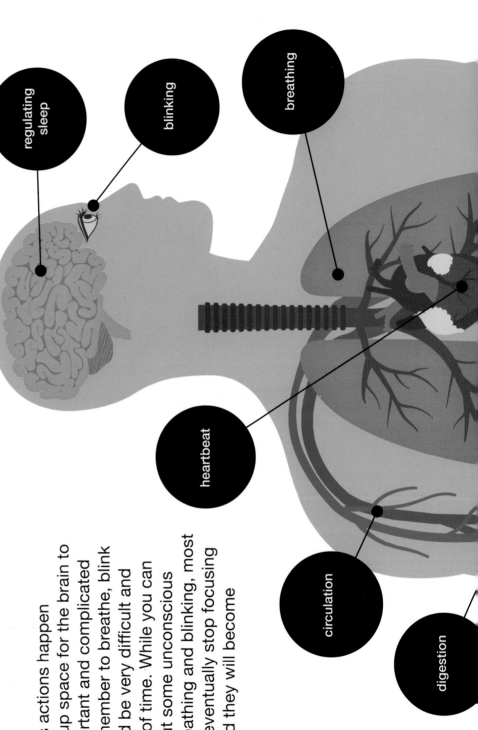

regulating sleep

blinking

breathing

heartbeat

circulation

digestion

Many unconscious actions are controlled by the brainstem. Instructions about unconscious actions go straight from the brainstem to different parts of the body, bypassing the rest of the brain.

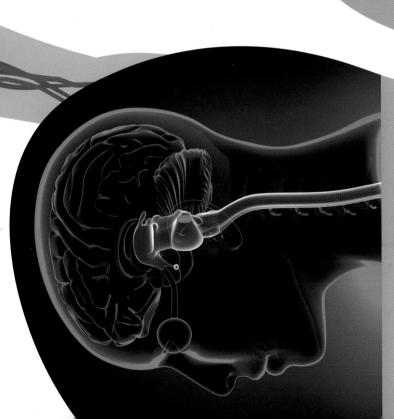

This computer-generated image shows the location of the brainstem. It connects the brain to the spinal cord.

Memory

Memory is the ability to store information so that it can be retrieved, or remembered, in the future. The brain is responsible for forming and storing memories.

Memories can be divided into different categories.

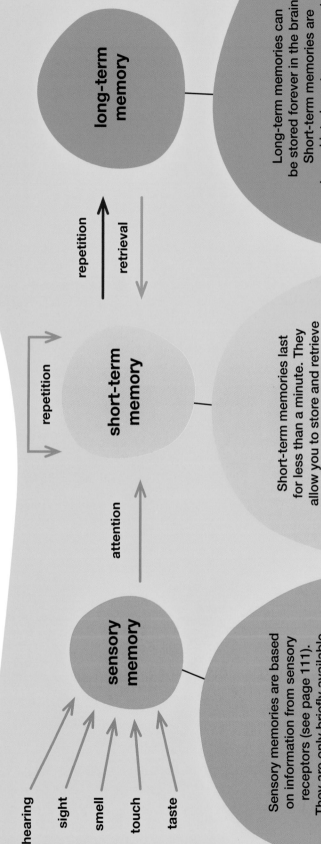

hearing
sight
smell
touch
taste

sensory memory

attention

short-term memory

repetition

repetition

retrieval

long-term memory

Sensory memories are based on information from sensory receptors (see page 111). They are only briefly available, but allow you to remember sounds, smells or sights even after the stimuli have stopped. If you pay particular attention to a sensory memory, it can become a short-term memory.

Short-term memories last for less than a minute. They allow you to store and retrieve information for a short period of time, such as repeating a telephone number that you have just heard. However, if short-term memories do not turn into long-term memories, they are forgotten forever.

Long-term memories can be stored forever in the brain. Short-term memories are turned into long-term memories through repetition and practising retrieving the information. Linking new information to existing long-term memories also helps to form new long-term memories. However, even long-term memories can be lost if they are not revisited occasionally.

30 seconds

the average duration of a short-term memory

The basal ganglia store memories of how to carry out processes, such as how to ride a bicycle.

The hippocampus converts short-term memories into long-term memories.

The brain organises and forms new long-term memories while you are asleep.

Different areas of the brain control different memory functions.

The amygdala is involved with converting short-term memories into long-term memories. It also links emotional responses to memories. These emotions can be triggered when the memory is recalled.

Conditions

There is a range of conditions and issues that affect the brain and nervous system. Some can be managed, while others can have a major impact on everyday life.

Epilepsy can be controlled with medication and by avoiding triggers that bring on seizures, such as stress, lack of sleep and flashing lights.

Epilepsy is a common brain condition. There is always electrical activity in the brain, as electrical signals travel along nerves. However, people with epilepsy experience sudden bursts of extreme electrical activity in the brain, called seizures. Seizures disrupt the way in which the brain works and can affect movement and consciousness. Some people are born with epilepsy, while others develop it as a result of an injury or an infection.

50 million

the number of people with epilepsy worldwide – the equivalent of the entire population of South Korea

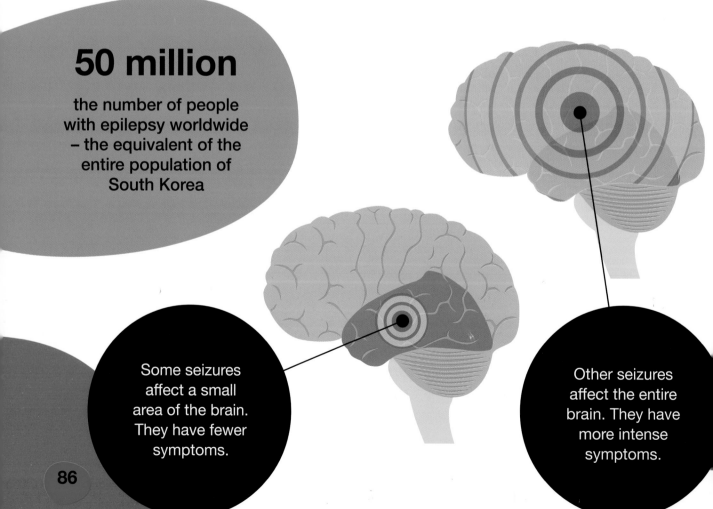

Some seizures affect a small area of the brain. They have fewer symptoms.

Other seizures affect the entire brain. They have more intense symptoms.

People who are involved in serious accidents sometimes experience spinal cord injuries. If the spinal cord is severed, messages can't travel to the spinal nerves beneath the break in the spinal cord. As a result, people with damaged spinal cords experience partial or total paralysis (loss of movement) in the parts of the body controlled by the nerves located below the break.

The location of the spinal cord injury affects how much of the body is paralysed.

If the top of the spinal cord breaks, the entire body from the neck down is affected.

A break in the upper back affects the arms, hands, chest and lower body.

A break at the bottom of the spinal cord affects the area below the waist.

If the spinal cord breaks in the middle of the back, the area from the chest down will be affected.

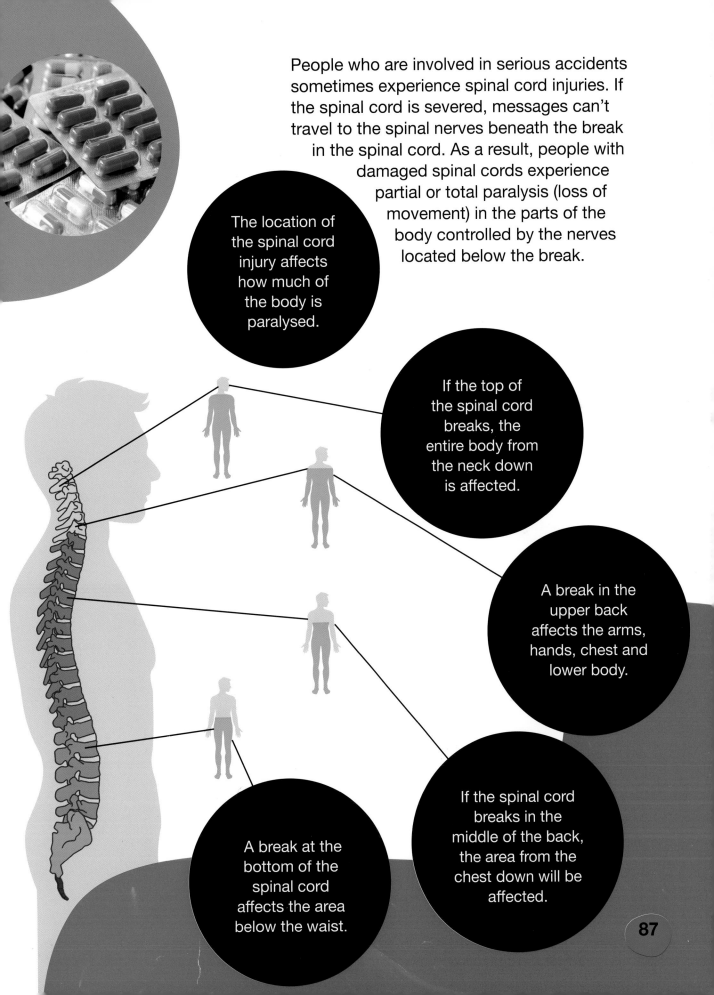

THE SENSES

The five main senses are sight, hearing, taste, smell and touch. They help us to understand our surroundings and keep us safe from danger.

Four of the five organs for sensing are in your head. These include the eyes (sight), the ears (hearing), the nose (smell) and the mouth (taste). Skin all over the body senses touch, but the most sensitive touch receptors are in your fingertips and palms.

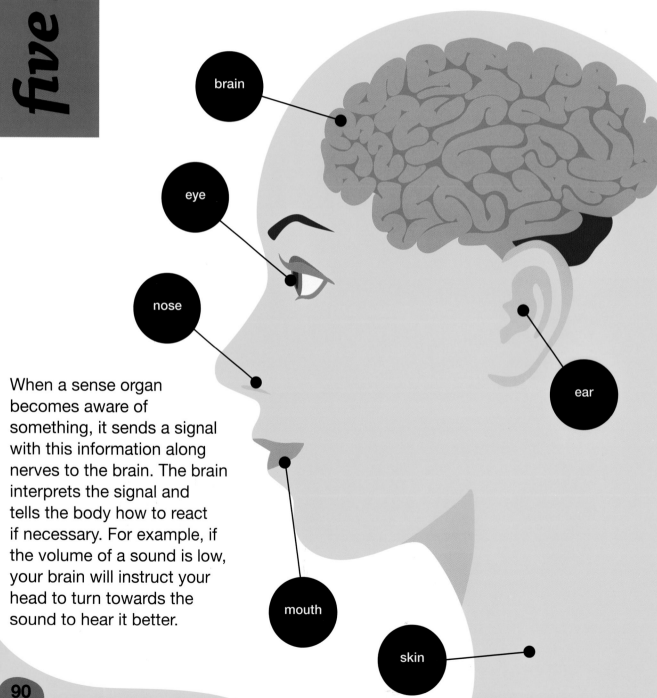

brain

eye

nose

ear

When a sense organ becomes aware of something, it sends a signal with this information along nerves to the brain. The brain interprets the signal and tells the body how to react if necessary. For example, if the volume of a sound is low, your brain will instruct your head to turn towards the sound to hear it better.

mouth

skin

The brain is constantly receiving information from the sense organs, so it blocks out any messages that aren't important. For example, our skin always senses the feeling of the clothes we wear, but the brain doesn't focus on this sensation unless it's important or different, such as an itch or discomfort.

Not everyone senses the same. Blind people, for example, sometimes find that their other senses, such as smell, are stronger than those of sighted people. This is because their brains develop in a different way to make up for their lack of sight.

11 million

the number of bits of information that the brain receives from the senses every second

Sight

Sight is the sense that we use the most to get information about our surroundings. Seeing begins when the eyes detect light. They send this information to the brain, where the light is understood as images.

The eyes are ball-shaped organs that sit in sockets in the head. From the outside, we can see the iris (coloured part), pupil (dark circle in the centre) and sclera (white outer coating), but there is much more to the eye inside the body.

The retina is the area where light-detecting cells are found.

The choroid contains arteries and veins to bring blood to and from the eye.

The optic nerve connects the eye to the brain.

The sclera protects the inside of the eye.

The vitreous body is a clear gel that fills the inside of the eye. It helps the eye to keep its shape.

The lens is the transparent internal part of the eye.

The cornea is the transparent front layer of the eye.

The pupil is actually a hole in the centre of the iris, although it looks like a dark circle.

The iris can be blue, green, brown or a combination of these colours.

80%

the percentage of the information we receive that comes through sight

Rods (in blue) are sensitive to black and white light and to dim light. They are used for night vision.

Cones (in pink) are sensitive to bright and coloured light.

The retina contains specialised receptor cells called rods and cones. Rods and cones are sensitive to different colours and strengths of light. When rods and cones sense light, they send information to the brain along the optic nerve. The brain interprets these signals, flips the image the right way around and understands what is being seen.

The process of seeing something begins when light reflects off an object and travels towards the eye.

Light rays cross over inside the eye. An upside-down version of the image is reflected on the retina.

Light goes into the eye through the lens, which focuses the light towards the retina at the back of the eye.

The cornea focuses the light so that it bends inwards to enter the eye.

dim light

bright light

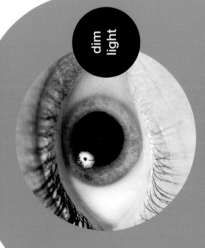

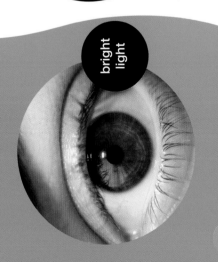

The pupil gets bigger or smaller depending on the amount of light. In dim light, the pupil gets bigger to let more light into the eye. In bright light, it gets smaller as less light is needed and too much light can be damaging.

93

Looking around

The structure and position of the eyes allow us to see beyond what is directly in front of us. They also give us a sense of depth to understand the position of objects.

Muscles around the eyes allow us to move them to different positions. This increases our field of vision (the area that we can see). We wouldn't normally be aware of objects above, below or to either side of our head, but we can see these areas if we move our eyes to different positions. There are limits, however, as we need to move our head to see objects behind us.

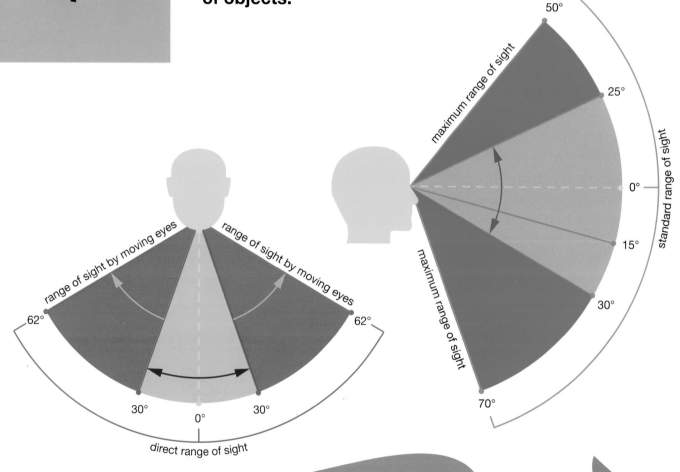

range of sight by moving eyes

range of sight by moving eyes

62°
62°
30°
0°
30°

direct range of sight

50°
25°
0°
15°
30°
70°

maximum range of sight
maximum range of sight
standard range of sight

nearly 360°

the field of vision of a rabbit, which helps them spot predators in all directions

Both eyes move when we look at an object to the side, but only the eye closest to that side can actually see the object.

Because our eyes are in different positions, each eye receives a slightly different image of objects in front of it. The brain combines these two versions into one single 3D image, in which we have a sense of depth. This is called binocular vision. It helps us to understand how close objects are to us, which is very important for actions, such as walking through a crowd, driving, throwing and catching.

binocular vision of the image created by the brain

image seen by left eye

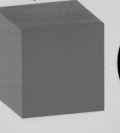

image seen by right eye

Hearing

Sound travels in waves of vibration. Organs inside the ear change these waves into signals that are sent on to the brain. The brain understands them as sounds or speech.

Sound waves travel down the ear canal to the middle ear. This area contains a thin membrane called an ear drum and three tiny bones called the incus, malleus and stapes. When sound waves hit the ear drum, it vibrates. The vibrations pass on to the tiny bones, which move as a result.

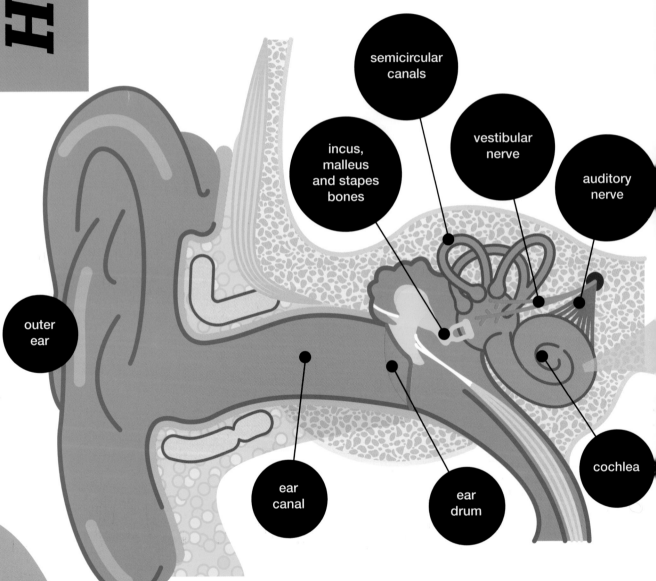

semicircular canals

incus, malleus and stapes bones

vestibular nerve

auditory nerve

outer ear

ear canal

ear drum

cochlea

The outer ear is outside the body. It has a gently funnelled shape that guides sound waves into the ear.

0.05 seconds

the amount of time it takes for someone to recognise a sound once it enters the ear, making hearing the fastest human sense

Vibrations from the middle ear travel on to the inner ear. The inner ear is deep inside the body. It contains the cochlea, semicircular canals (see page 109) and nerves that go to the brain. The cochlea is a spiral-shaped organ, filled with fluid. Inside the cochlea is a section called the organ of Corti, which has sensitive hair receptor cells on its walls. When the hair receptor cells sense vibrations, they convert this information into an electrical signal. The signal travels from the cochlea to the brain along the cochlear nerve.

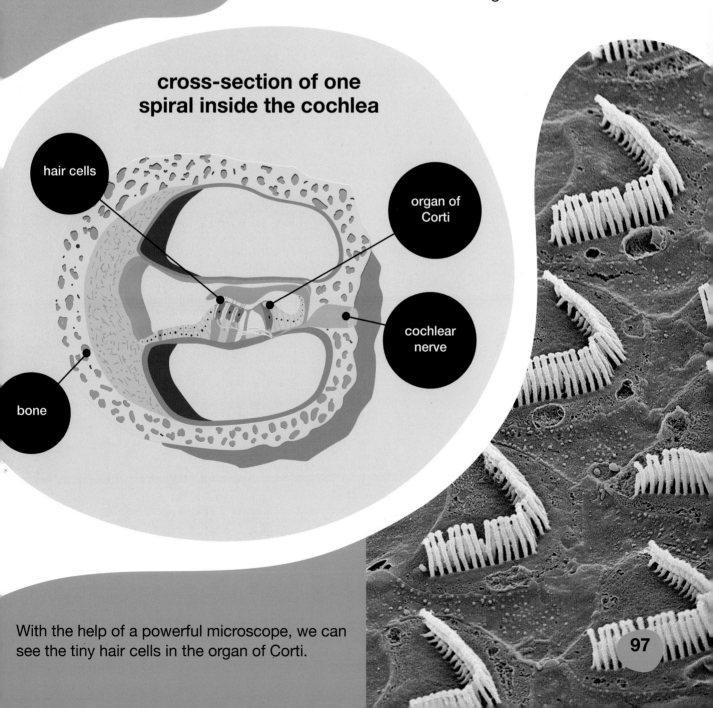

cross-section of one spiral inside the cochlea

hair cells

organ of Corti

cochlear nerve

bone

With the help of a powerful microscope, we can see the tiny hair cells in the organ of Corti.

Different sounds

There are many types of sound – loud and quiet, high and low. However, the range of human hearing is limited, and we can't hear every sound.

Sound waves are different for high- and low-pitched sounds, as well as for loud and quiet sounds. We can see these differences if we track the vibrations on a machine.

The louder a sound, the more energy it has. Loud sounds make tall waves with a high amplitude (distance from the rest position to the top of the wave). Quiet sounds have less energy, so they result in short waves with low amplitude.

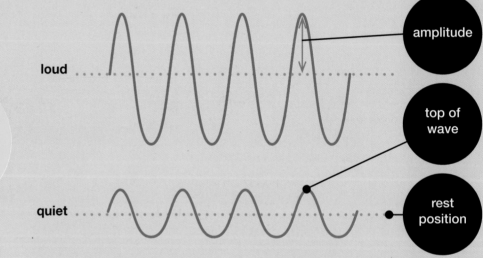

loud

amplitude

top of wave

quiet

rest position

Pitch is how high or low a sound is. It affects the speed of vibration. High-pitched sounds come from quick vibrations, in which the waves are close together. Low-pitched sounds come from slow vibrations, in which the waves are far apart.

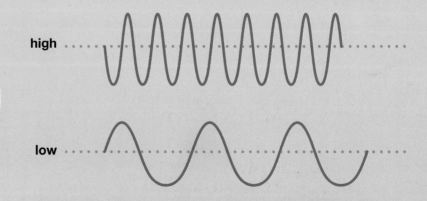

high

There are some high and low pitches that humans can't hear because the cochlea isn't sensitive enough. There are also sounds that are too quiet for us to hear. We must avoid very loud sounds, as they can damage our hearing.

Loudness is measured in decibels (dB). People with hearing loss (see page 115) may not be able to hear sounds at the lower end of the scale.

It is important to wear ear defenders to protect your ears from loud noises if you are working with noisy machines.

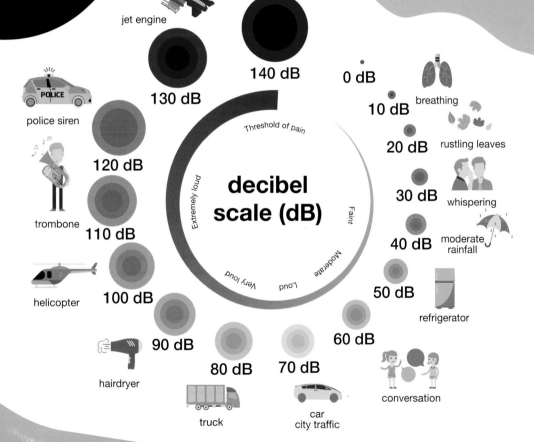

jet engine

fireworks

140 dB

130 dB

0 dB

10 dB   breathing

police siren

20 dB   rustling leaves

120 dB

Threshold of pain

30 dB   whispering

trombone

decibel scale (dB)

Extremely loud   Faint

40 dB   moderate rainfall

110 dB

Moderate

50 dB

Very loud   Loud

helicopter

100 dB

refrigerator

90 dB

60 dB

hairdryer

80 dB   70 dB

conversation

truck

car city traffic

20,000 hertz (Hz)

the highest pitched sounds that humans can hear, compared to the maximum 150,000 Hz that dolphins can hear

Taste

The sense of taste happens in the mouth. As well as bringing us pleasure through eating, the sense of taste also helps to protect the body. It warns us against poisonous or rotten foods that may make us ill.

The tongue is covered with thousands of tiny bumps called papillae (singular papilla). On each papilla are hundreds of taste buds. Taste buds contain taste receptor cells that recognise different chemicals in food. The inner cheeks, inside of the lips, back and roof of the mouth are also covered in taste buds.

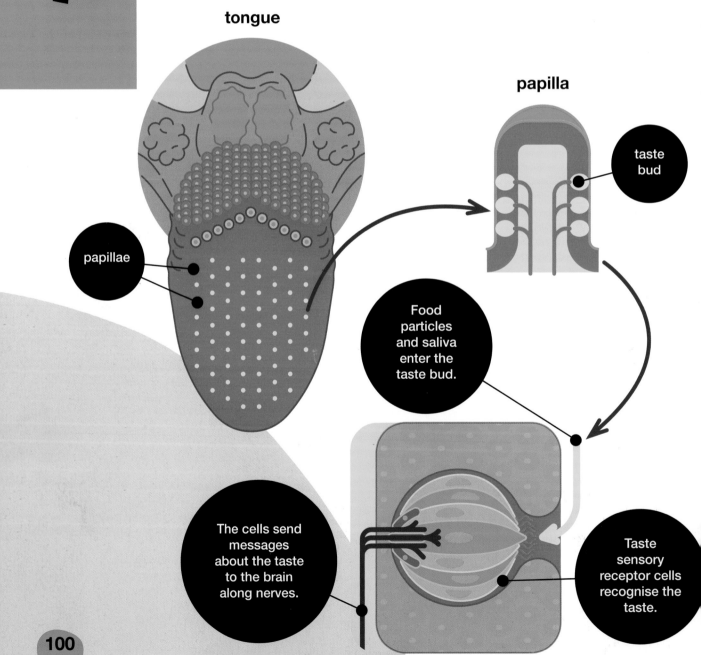

tongue

papilla

papillae

taste bud

Food particles and saliva enter the taste bud.

The cells send messages about the taste to the brain along nerves.

Taste sensory receptor cells recognise the taste.

The papillae on the tongue can be seen with the naked eye.

There are five basic tastes – sweet, sour, salty, bitter and umami (rich and savoury). A combination of these tastes, along with smell, determines the flavour of food. Many poisonous foods are bitter, so humans have developed a dislike for very bitter flavours. Strong sour tastes can also be unpleasant and are often a sign that food is rotten.

sweet

honey

ripe banana

sour

lemon

plain yoghurt

salty

crisps

cured foods, such as salami

bitter

dark chocolate

olives

umami

cheese

soy sauce

2,000–8,000

the number of taste buds on the tongue – the huge variation in number of taste buds is one reason people have different taste preferences

Smell

Our sense of smell allows us to identify millions of different smells. Some are pleasant, while others, such as poisonous gases and rotten stenches, are warnings.

Some objects release odour molecules that transmit their smell. These molecules are very small and light, so they float easily through the air. We breathe them in accidentally or on purpose when we sniff through our nose. The odour molecules travel through the nostrils into the nose.

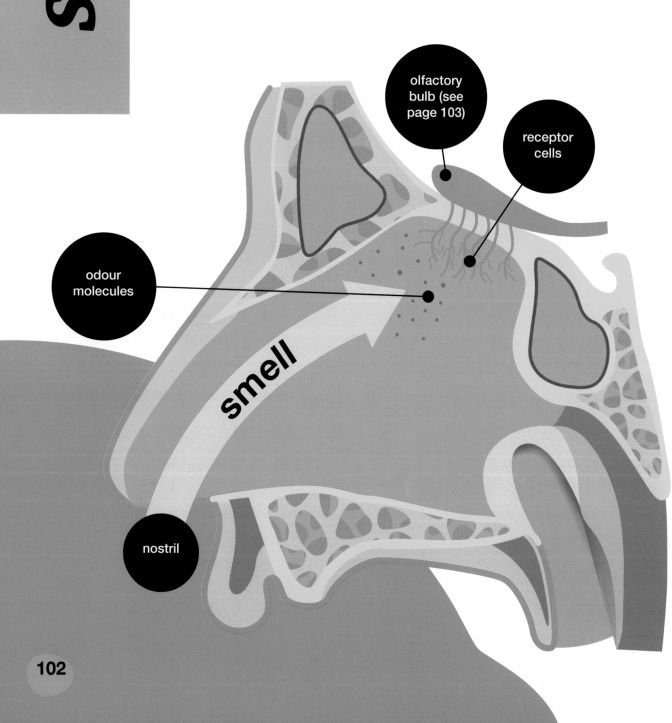

olfactory bulb (see page 103)

receptor cells

odour molecules

smell

nostril

Smell receptor cells are found inside the nose at the top of each nostril. The cells have special hair-like endings called cilia, which recognise odour molecules and send a message to an area known as the olfactory bulb. The olfactory bulb passes these messages on to the brain, where they are understood as smells.

olfactory bulb

nerve cells

odour molecules

smell receptor cells

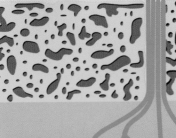
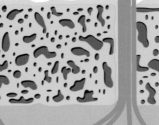
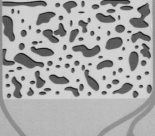
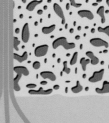

10,000

the number of times more sensitive the sense of smell is than the sense of taste

When you have a cold, you lose some of your sense of smell because your nose is blocked and odour molecules cannot reach the receptor cells. Smell also contributes to your sense of taste, which is why taste is affected when you have a cold.

Touch

Our skin gives us lots of information about the world around us. It contains special touch receptor cells that recognise texture, pressure, temperature and pain.

The skin is made up of three main layers. The outer layer is called the epidermis, the middle layer is called the dermis and the bottom layer is called the hypodermis.

The epidermis is a barrier that stops bacteria and viruses from entering the body. It also contains tiny holes called pores through which sweat leaves the body.

Blood vessels and most touch receptor cells are found in the dermis. It also contains the roots of the hairs that cover our skin, and sweat glands that produce sweat.

The hypodermis contains a layer of fat that helps to keep the body warm. This fat can be burned if we need extra energy.

All of our skin contains touch receptor cells, but they are most concentrated in certain areas, such as the fingertips and the lips. Some receptor cells are close to the surface, while others are found deeper down. Different types of receptor cell are sensitive to different kinds of touch.

slow vibrations

touch and pressure

pain and temperature (see pages 74–75)

stretching of the skin

cold temperatures

pressure and fast vibrations

touch

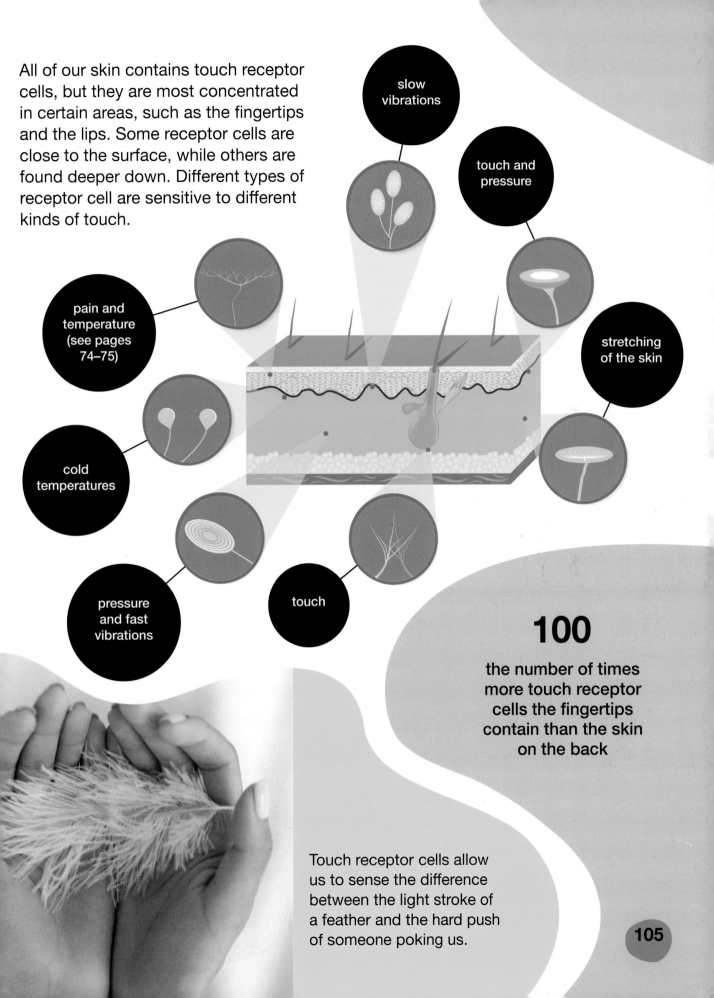

100

the number of times more touch receptor cells the fingertips contain than the skin on the back

Touch receptor cells allow us to sense the difference between the light stroke of a feather and the hard push of someone poking us.

Sensing pain

The feeling of pain alerts us to danger. Discomfort lets us know that something is wrong so that we can react and try to stop things from hurting us.

Pain touch receptors aren't only found in the skin – they are also located inside the body in internal organs, muscles and joints. They sense damage done to different parts of the body through injury, illness or infection. We experience this damage as pain, such as a stomach ache or a sore muscle. Other dangers that can harm the body create different sensations.

low temperatures – freezing sensation

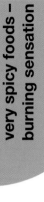

very spicy foods – burning sensation

high temperatures – burning sensation

some poisons – itchy sensation

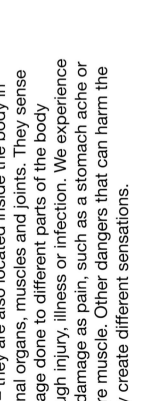

When you get a cut, the pressure of the object that creates the cut alerts pressure receptor cells. They inform the brain that the skin has been damaged.

Some pain receptor cells trigger reflexes – involuntary and very quick reactions. For example, if you touch something very hot, your hand pulls away as a reflex. Unlike other sensory messages that go via the brain (see pages 90–91), reflex reactions take a shortcut. They bypass the brain and go straight from the receptor cell to the muscles via the spinal cord. This saves time so that the body is protected more quickly.

200

the number of pain receptors in 1 square cm of skin, compared to 15 pressure receptors, 6 cold receptors and only 1 warmth receptor

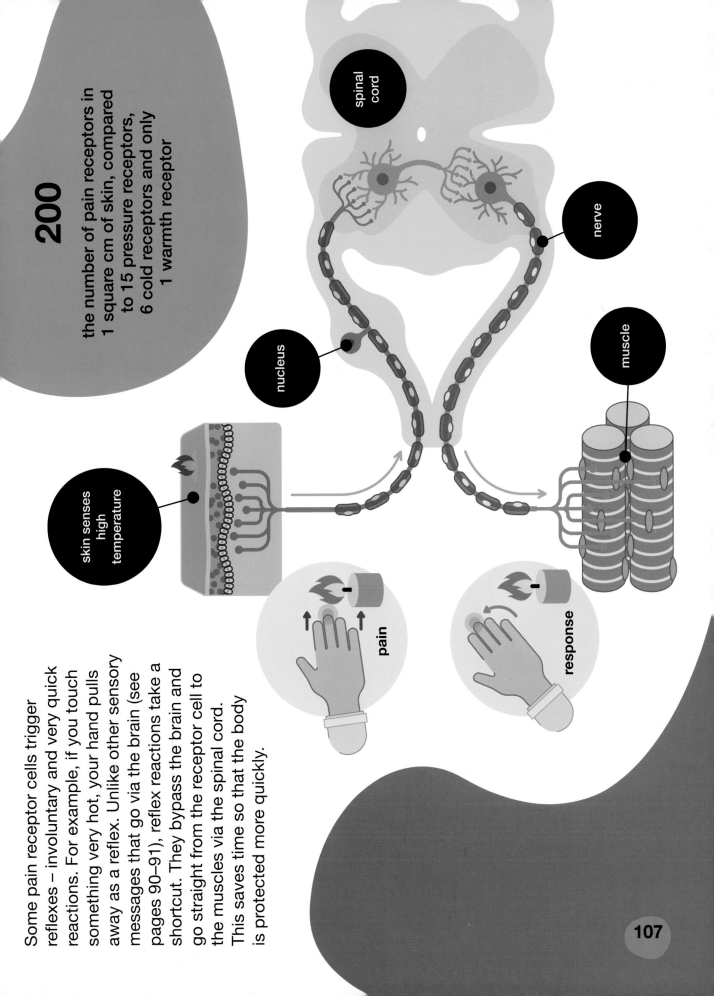

spinal cord

nerve

nucleus

muscle

skin senses high temperature

pain

response

Position and balance

When thinking about the senses, people often forget the awareness of movement, position of the body and the sense of balance. However, these are very important senses.

Proprioception is the sense of knowing where your body is and its position in relation to its environment. Sensory receptor cells in muscles and joints send signals to the brain to give it information about the position of the body without having to look to see where it is. For example, if you close your eyes, you can still touch your nose. This is because your body knows the position of your nose and your arm, and reacts to guide the hand to the nose as it moves through the air. Proprioception allows us to move quickly and easily without having to think about it.

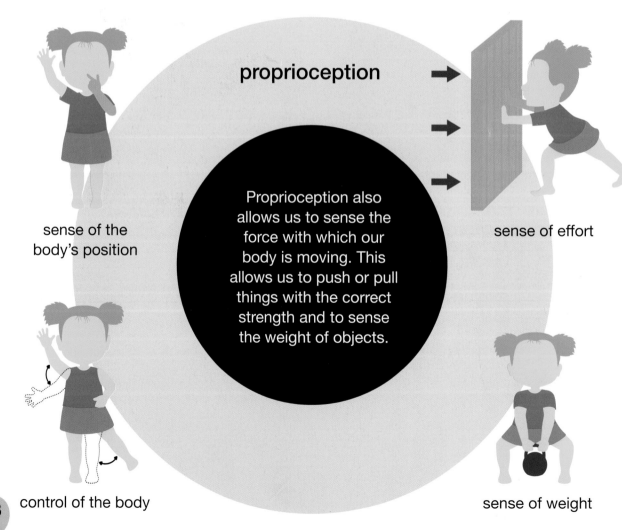

proprioception

Proprioception also allows us to sense the force with which our body is moving. This allows us to push or pull things with the correct strength and to sense the weight of objects.

sense of the body's position

sense of effort

control of the body

sense of weight

Balance is also related to sense, as sensors in the ears react to changes in position to keep the body upright. These sensors are located in a set of tubes in the inner ear called the semicircular canals. When you move your body, liquid in the tubes moves and bends tiny hairs inside an area called the cupula. The hairs are connected to nerves that send messages to the brain along the vestibular nerve. These messages inform the brain of the position of the body, so that it can instruct the body to move to keep its balance if necessary.

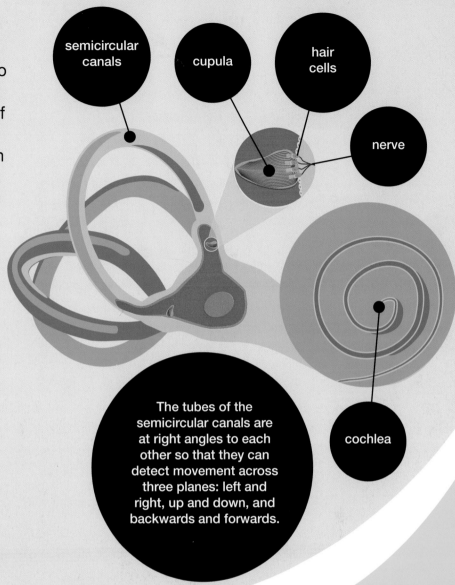

semicircular canals

cupula

hair cells

nerve

cochlea

The tubes of the semicircular canals are at right angles to each other so that they can detect movement across three planes: left and right, up and down, and backwards and forwards.

12–22 mm

the average length of each semicircular canal

Spinning around makes you feel dizzy because the movement makes the liquid in the semicircular tubes slosh around. This sends many signals to the brain, which take a while to be interpreted. This produces a dizzy feeling.

Reacting to senses

Information from receptor cells in the sensory organs travels along nerves to the brain. The brain interprets the information and reacts, if necessary, by sending out messages to parts of the body through the nervous system.

The four sensory organs on the face (the ears, eyes, nose and mouth) send information straight into the brainstem (a part of the brain) along cranial nerves in the head. Other sensory cells, such as those in the skin, send information along long nerves in the body. The information goes into the spinal cord and then travels up into the brain.

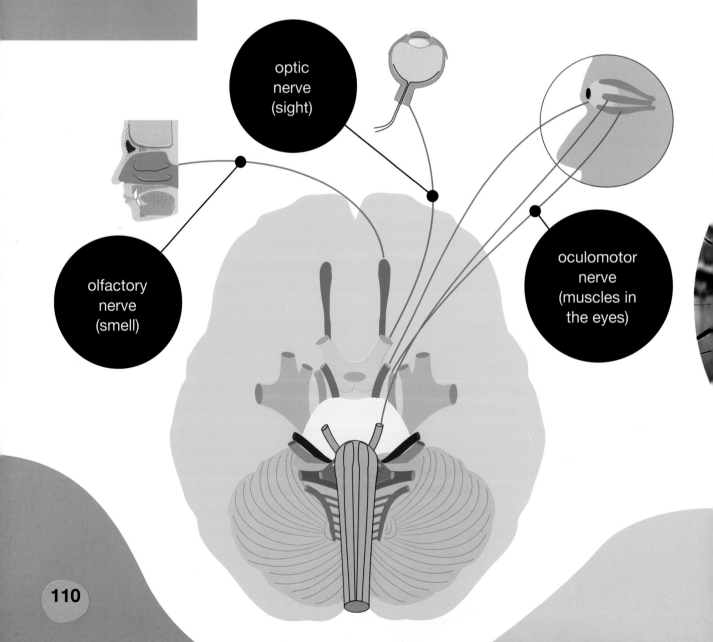

optic nerve (sight)

olfactory nerve (smell)

oculomotor nerve (muscles in the eyes)

Different kinds of neurones (nerve cells) carry signals to and from the brain. Sensory neurones carry signals from sensory receptors to the brain. Motor neurones carry signals from the brain to muscles and glands in the body. They instruct these parts of the body to react based on information from the senses, such as instructing the salivary glands to start producing saliva when you smell something delicious.

motor neurone

muscle

sensory neurone

receptor cell

approx. 60 km

the length of the nerves in the human body if they were joined together

Nerve cells are connected to each other in a network across the body. Along with the brain and spinal cord, they make up the nervous system.

Internal senses

As well as the five main senses that let us know what is going on outside our body, we also rely on internal senses to give us information about what is going on inside the body.

Chemical receptors in different parts of the body monitor the levels of chemicals in the blood. For example, if you stop breathing, or aren't breathing enough, chemical receptors in the blood vessels detect that there isn't enough oxygen in the blood (or that there is too much carbon dioxide). You experience feelings of dizziness and suffocation and you know it is important to start breathing again.

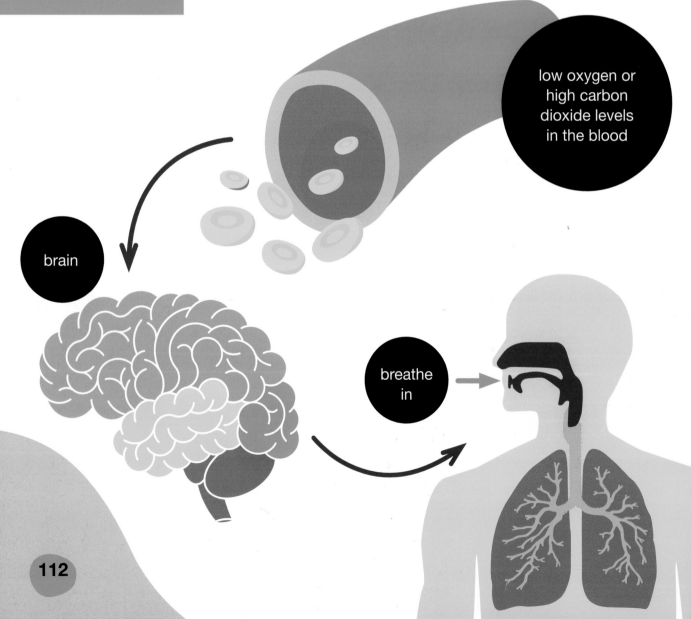

low oxygen or high carbon dioxide levels in the blood

brain

breathe in

You may have experienced feelings of dizziness when your breath runs out underwater. This lets you know that you need to come back to the surface to breathe.

Some internal organs send messages to the brain to report when they are full.

brain

stomach

As food fills the stomach, sensors in the walls of the stomach feel it stretching and send messages to the brain. The brain helps to create a feeling of fullness so that we know to stop eating. The feeling of fullness also comes from hormones released by the small intestine during digestion.

20 minutes

the approximate amount of time it takes for the body to feel full once you start to eat

When the bladder and rectum are full of urine and faeces, sensors in their walls send a message to the brain. The brain creates the sensation that we need to go to the toilet.

bladder

rectum

113

Problems with senses

People can have issues with any of the senses, but sight and hearing issues are the most common. In some cases they can be treated with glasses, surgery or devices, such as hearing aids and implants.

Two common problems with sight are short- and long-sightedness. A short-sighted person will see close objects clearly, but distant objects will be blurry, while a long-sighted person has the opposite problem. These issues are caused by a problem with the shape of the eye, which means that light can't focus properly on the retina. They can be treated with glasses or by changing the shape of the cornea with lasers.

People who are short-sighted have eyeballs that are too long. This means that light rays focus in front of the retina, making objects appear blurry.

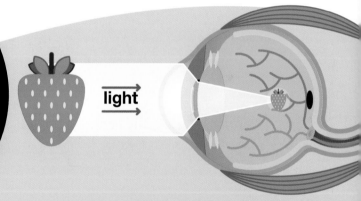

People who are long-sighted have eyeballs that are too short. This means that light rays focus behind the retina, making objects appear blurry.

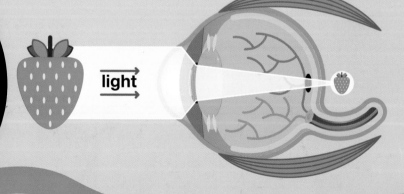

Cataracts are another common sight problem, especially among elderly people. The lens becomes cloudy, which can reduce vision. Cataracts are caused by many factors including smoking, injury to the eye and old age.

Some people are born deaf or with hearing loss, while others lose their hearing as the result of an injury or illness. Our hearing also gets worse as we get older, as the sensory cells in our ears are damaged over time. Standard hearing aids can help some people with mild hearing loss to hear more.

For people with severe hearing loss, a device such as a cochlear implant may be necessary. A cochlear implant converts sound waves into electrical signals that go straight to the auditory nerve and on to the brain, bypassing the body's hearing system. Some people in the deaf community choose not to use any devices that help with hearing. They communicate via sign language or lip reading.

An external transmitter receives information about sounds from the speech processor and turns it into electrical signals.

Electrodes stimulate the auditory nerve, sending electrical signals along the nerve to the brain, where they are understood as sounds.

The external microphone picks up sound waves.

Electrical signals are sent from the receiver to a group of electrodes in the cochlea.

The internal receiver picks up signals from the transmitter.

A speech processor filters sounds to focus on speech.

466 million

the number of people worldwide with some degree of hearing loss, which is 5 per cent of the global population

THE DIGESTIVE SYSTEM

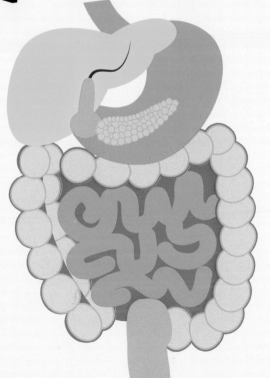

Your digestive system

Your digestive system breaks down food so that the body can use it. Energy from food is used to power cells in the body. Food also contains nutrients that help with important processes in the body, such as cell growth and repair, keeping bones healthy, and supporting the immune system.

The digestive system begins in the mouth. It continues through the body via the stomach and intestines, and ends at the anus (bottom). In the mouth and stomach, food is broken down into very small pieces so that the body can absorb it.

9 metres

the length of the digestive system from the mouth to the anus, which is almost the length of a bus

oesophagus

stomach

mouth

liver

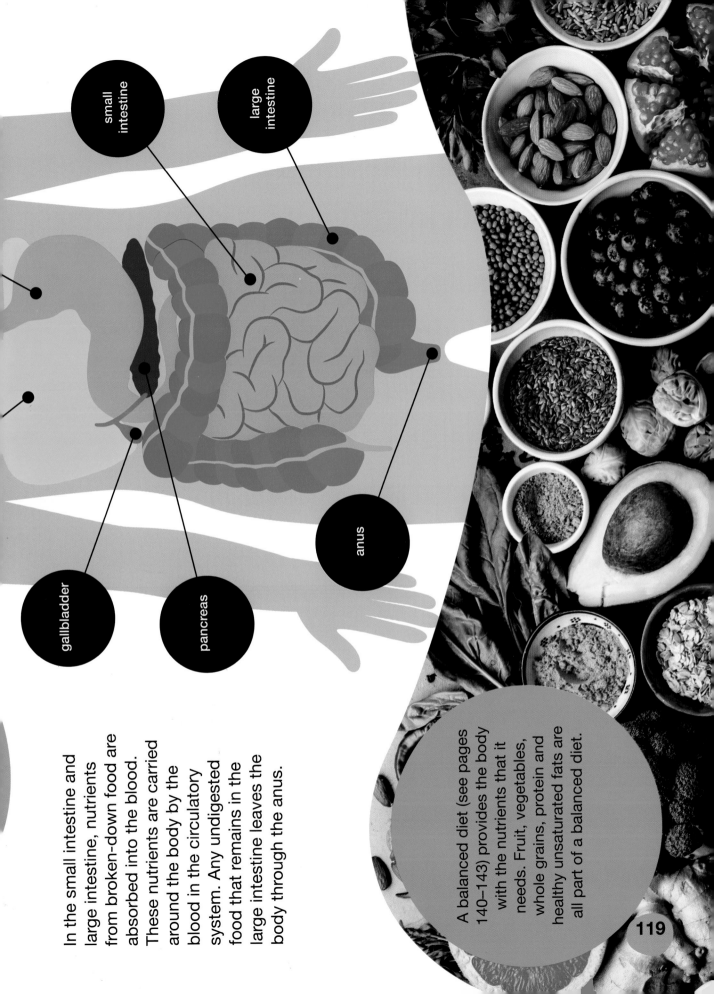

small intestine

large intestine

gallbladder

pancreas

anus

In the small intestine and large intestine, nutrients from broken-down food are absorbed into the blood. These nutrients are carried around the body by the blood in the circulatory system. Any undigested food that remains in the large intestine leaves the body through the anus.

A balanced diet (see pages 140–143) provides the body with the nutrients that it needs. Fruit, vegetables, whole grains, protein and healthy unsaturated fats are all part of a balanced diet.

Digestion starts in the mouth. The teeth begin to mechanically break down food, while enzymes in saliva (spit) break down food chemically.

Teeth cut and tear food apart. Each type of tooth breaks down food in a different way. Incisors (at the front) cut, while canines (in the front corners) grip and tear food. Premolars and molars (at the back) crush and grind food.

incisors

canines

premolars

molars

Before and during eating, saliva is released into the mouth from glands located in the cheeks and under the tongue. Saliva moistens the mouth and throat, and prevents them from being damaged by food. It also sticks chewed food together into a bolus (ball) that can easily be swallowed.

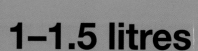

1–1.5 litres

the average amount of saliva produced by an adult every day

how food is swallowed

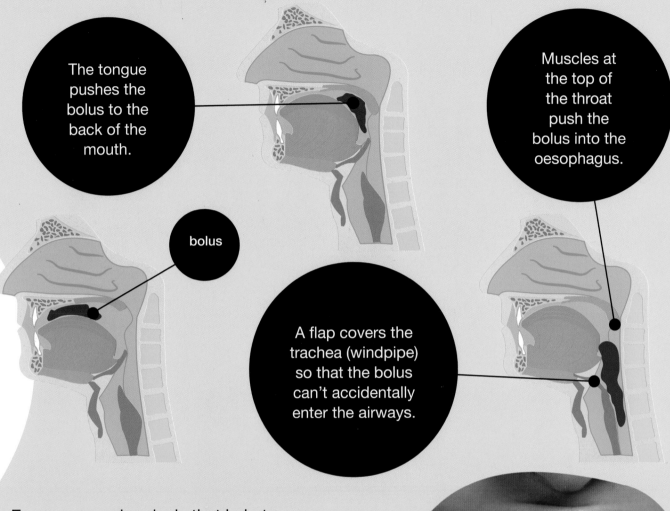

The tongue pushes the bolus to the back of the mouth.

bolus

Muscles at the top of the throat push the bolus into the oesophagus.

A flap covers the trachea (windpipe) so that the bolus can't accidentally enter the airways.

Enzymes are chemicals that help to break down substances, such as food. Different types of enzymes are needed to break down each type of food so that it can be absorbed (see page 141). The enzymes used in digestion are released in different parts of the digestive system. In the mouth, enzymes break down carbohydrates.

Muscles in the tongue move food around the mouth. The tongue is the only muscle in the human body that is not supported by a bone.

121

The oesophagus is a 25-cm-long tube that connects the mouth to the stomach. When food is swallowed, muscles in the wall of the oesophagus push it down to the stomach.

When a bolus is swallowed and passes into the oesophagus, muscles above the bolus, at the top of the oesophagus, contract. At the same time, the muscles underneath the bolus relax, creating space for the bolus to move down into. This process of contracting and relaxing muscles is called peristalsis.

peristalsis

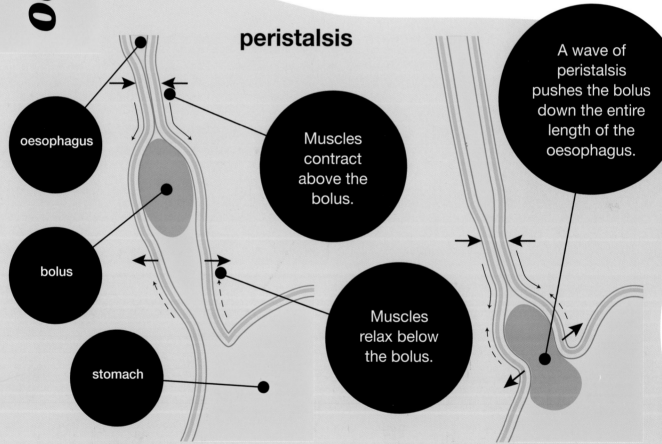

oesophagus

bolus

stomach

Muscles contract above the bolus.

Muscles relax below the bolus.

A wave of peristalsis pushes the bolus down the entire length of the oesophagus.

10 seconds

the amount of time it takes for food to travel down the oesophagus to the stomach, beginning from the start of a swallow

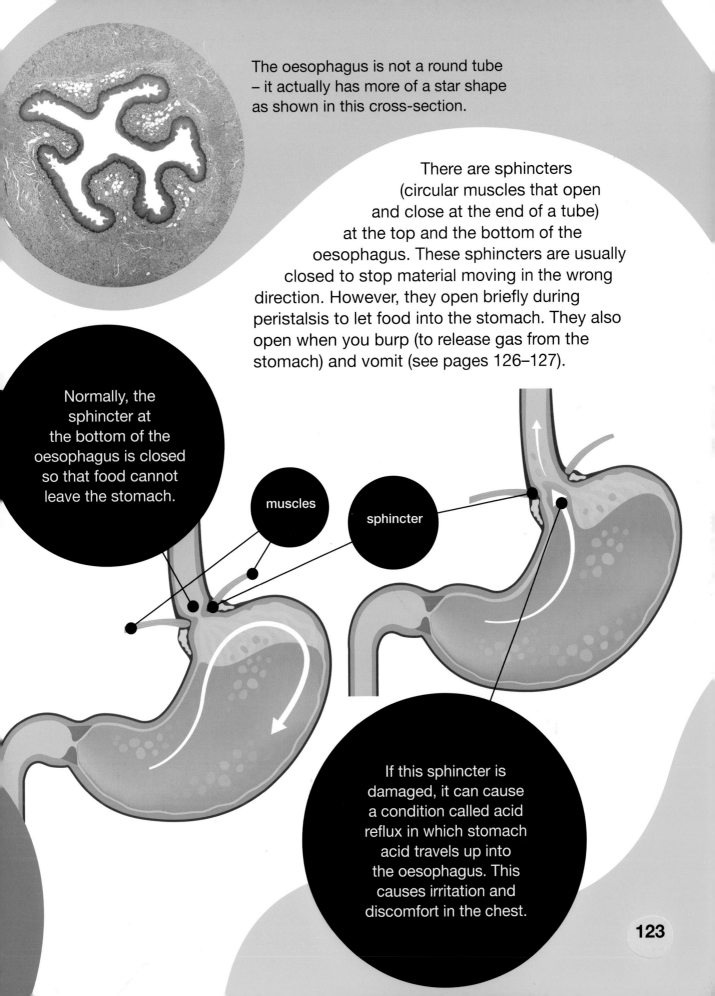

The oesophagus is not a round tube – it actually has more of a star shape as shown in this cross-section.

There are sphincters (circular muscles that open and close at the end of a tube) at the top and the bottom of the oesophagus. These sphincters are usually closed to stop material moving in the wrong direction. However, they open briefly during peristalsis to let food into the stomach. They also open when you burp (to release gas from the stomach) and vomit (see pages 126–127).

Normally, the sphincter at the bottom of the oesophagus is closed so that food cannot leave the stomach.

muscles

sphincter

If this sphincter is damaged, it can cause a condition called acid reflux in which stomach acid travels up into the oesophagus. This causes irritation and discomfort in the chest.

Food passes from the oesophagus into the stomach. The stomach is a sack of muscle where both mechanical and chemical digestion take place.

In the stomach, food is broken down further into a mushy liquid called chyme. This is done in several ways, including:

- Muscles in the stomach wall contract, churning the food and breaking it down.
- Enzymes in the stomach break down protein particles.

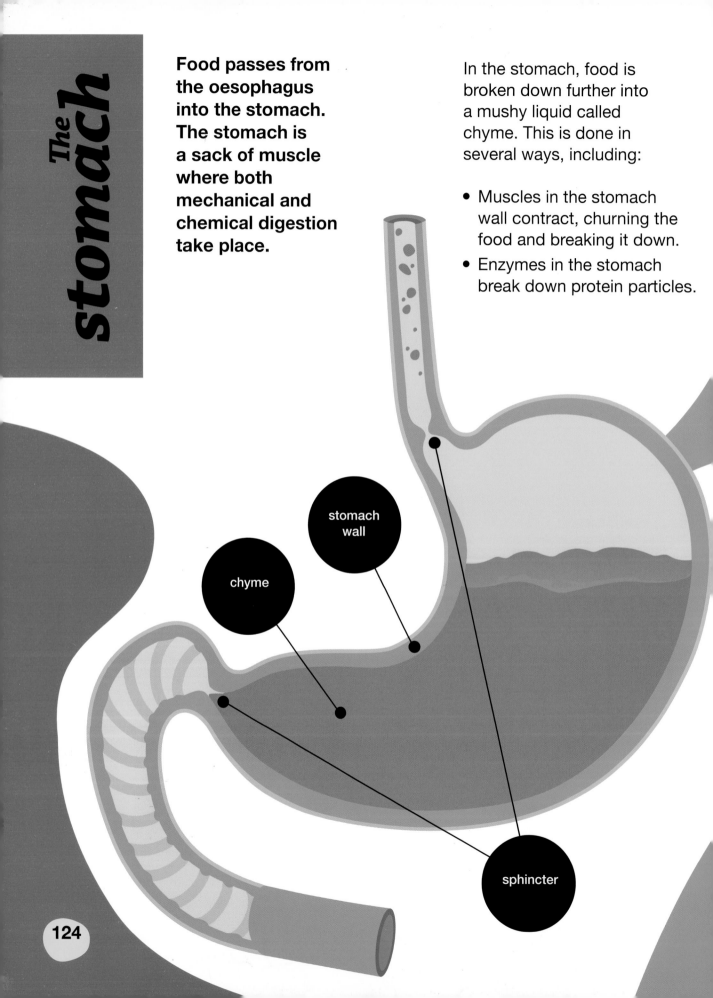

stomach wall

chyme

sphincter

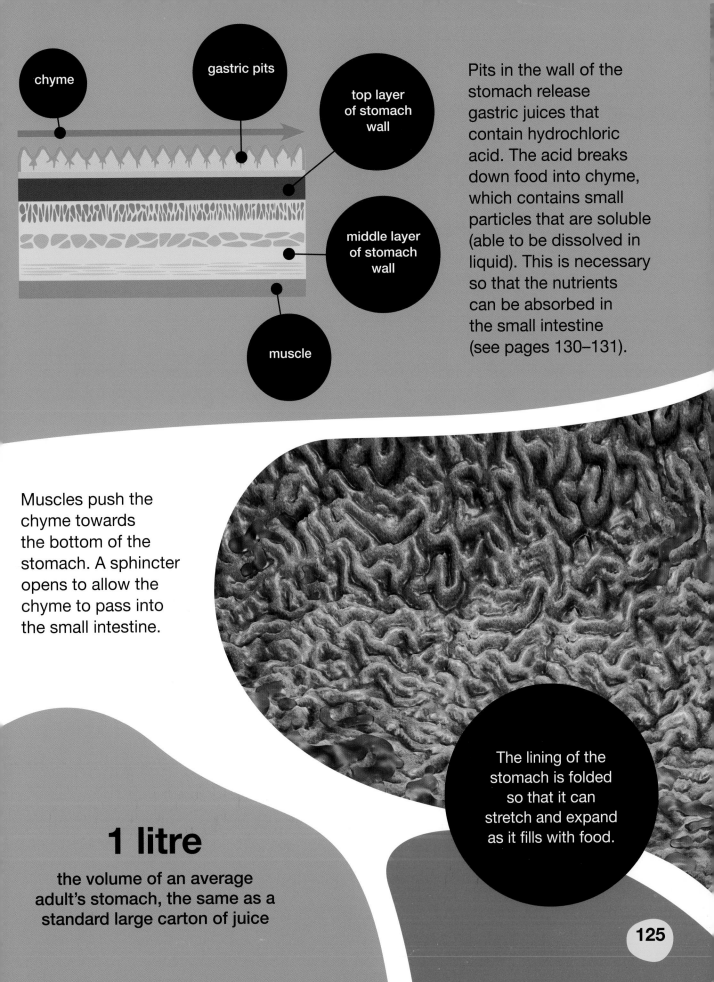

chyme

gastric pits

top layer of stomach wall

middle layer of stomach wall

muscle

Pits in the wall of the stomach release gastric juices that contain hydrochloric acid. The acid breaks down food into chyme, which contains small particles that are soluble (able to be dissolved in liquid). This is necessary so that the nutrients can be absorbed in the small intestine (see pages 130–131).

Muscles push the chyme towards the bottom of the stomach. A sphincter opens to allow the chyme to pass into the small intestine.

The lining of the stomach is folded so that it can stretch and expand as it fills with food.

1 litre

the volume of an average adult's stomach, the same as a standard large carton of juice

Vomiting

When you vomit, the contents of the stomach are forced back up the oesophagus and out of the mouth. Vomiting can happen for many different reasons, including illness and food poisoning.

First, the sphincter at the top of the stomach opens.

Just before vomiting, the body prepares itself. Salivary glands release extra saliva to protect the teeth from acidic stomach juices. The lungs take a breath in so that there is less risk of breathing in vomit later.

Then, peristalsis happens in reverse. Muscles contract and relax in a wave, moving up the oesophagus to force the vomit upwards and out of the mouth.

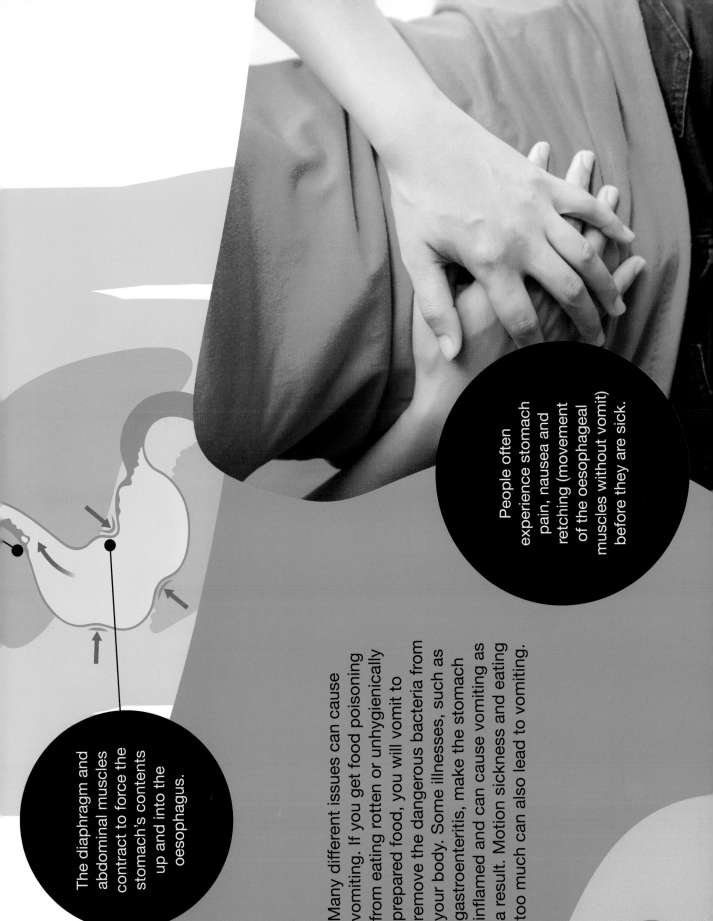

The diaphragm and abdominal muscles contract to force the stomach's contents up and into the oesophagus.

People often experience stomach pain, nausea and retching (movement of the oesophageal muscles without vomit) before they are sick.

Many different issues can cause vomiting. If you get food poisoning from eating rotten or unhygienically prepared food, you will vomit to remove the dangerous bacteria from your body. Some illnesses, such as gastroenteritis, make the stomach inflamed and can cause vomiting as a result. Motion sickness and eating too much can also lead to vomiting.

The liver and pancreas

The digestive system is supported by the liver, the pancreas and the gallbladder. These organs carry out important roles in the digestive process.

The liver sits beside the stomach, underneath the diaphragm. It produces a substance called bile, which breaks down the fat in food. The liver also filters waste from the blood and helps to break down food nutrients into substances that the body needs. The liver is the only internal organ that can grow back if damaged. As little as 25 per cent of a liver can grow back into a full organ.

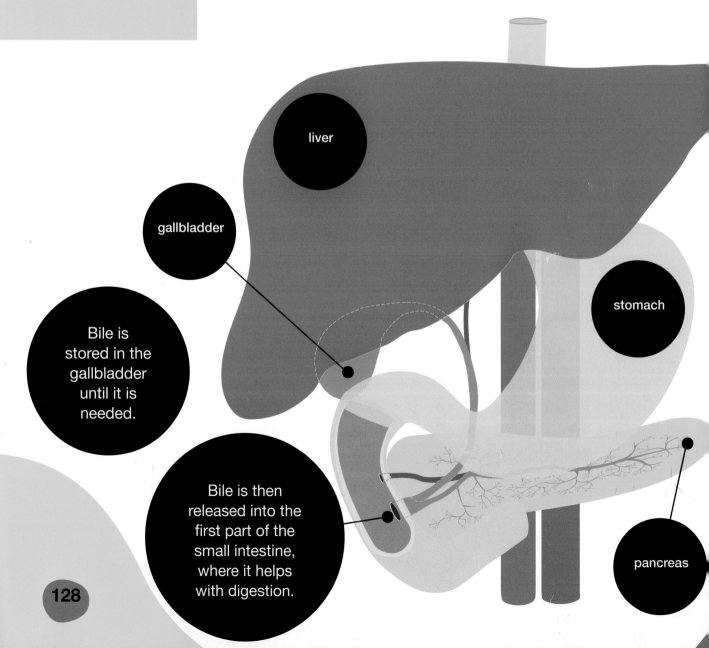

liver

gallbladder

stomach

Bile is stored in the gallbladder until it is needed.

Bile is then released into the first part of the small intestine, where it helps with digestion.

pancreas

The pancreas is a small organ behind the stomach. It makes digestive enzymes that break down carbohydrates, proteins and fats. These enzymes are released into the opening of the small intestine. The pancreas also helps to control the amount of sugar in the blood by releasing a hormone called insulin into the bloodstream. Insulin helps cells to absorb sugar for energy.

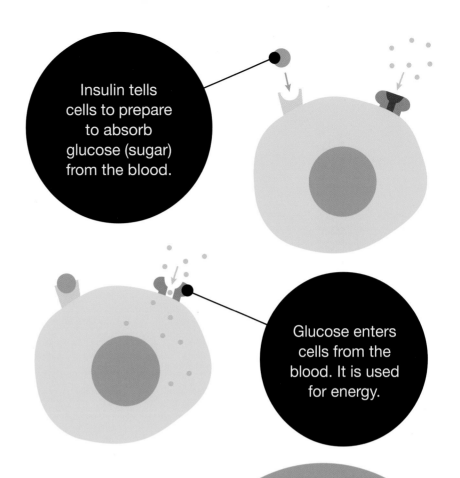

Insulin tells cells to prepare to absorb glucose (sugar) from the blood.

Glucose enters cells from the blood. It is used for energy.

1.5 kg

the average weight of an adult's liver – the weight of a small chihuahua

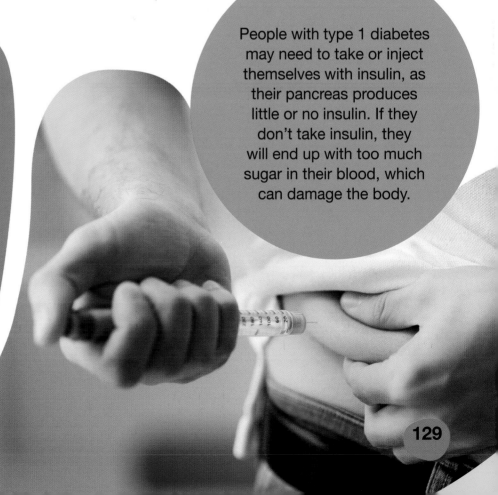

People with type 1 diabetes may need to take or inject themselves with insulin, as their pancreas produces little or no insulin. If they don't take insulin, they will end up with too much sugar in their blood, which can damage the body.

The small intestine

The small intestine is a long, narrow tube, measuring around 7 m in length. Here, most of the nutrients from digested food are absorbed into the bloodstream.

The small intestine can be divided into three parts – the duodenum, the jejunum and the ileum. It takes about three to six hours for food to pass through the entire small intestine. Muscles in the walls of the small intestine push chyme along by peristalsis, and squeeze it to break it down further.

The duodenum connects to the stomach. Here, enzymes from the liver and pancreas mix with the chyme, breaking down the nutrients into tiny molecules.

The jejenum is the middle section of the small intestine. The molecules from broken-down nutrients in food are absorbed into the bloodstream here.

The ileum is the end of the small intestine. Any remaining molecules are absorbed into the blood here. Any undigested food passes through the ileum into the large intestine.

large intestine

Absorption of nutrients from food takes place through the walls of the small intestine. When the chyme touches the small intestine walls, tiny broken-down molecules from food pass through the thin intestinal walls and enter the bloodstream. The walls of the small intestine are folded and lined with a vast number of tiny projections called villi. This increases the surface area of the small intestine so that there is a much larger space for absorption to take place.

Nutrients pass into the bloodstream. Blood vessels carry nutrients to the rest of the body.

Blood vessels bring blood into each villus (singular of villi).

Nutrients pass through the walls of the villi.

This computer-generated image shows the walls of the small intestine, covered with millions of villi.

250 square metres

the surface area of the small intestine, which is around the same size as a tennis court

The large intestine

Any undigested remains of chyme, such as fibre, pass from the small intestine into the large intestine. The large intestine is shorter and wider than the small intestine, measuring only about 1.5 m long.

Muscles in the walls of the large intestine push undigested chyme along. Water, salt and vitamins are absorbed through the intestinal walls, which are smooth, unlike the walls of the small intestine. As water is absorbed from the chyme, any remaining undigested matter dries out. The movement of the muscle walls compacts this matter into solid faeces (see pages 134–135).

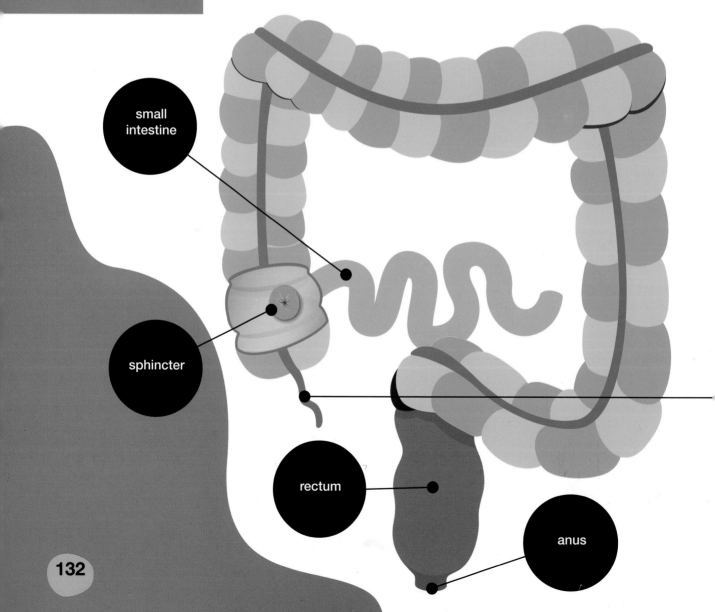

small intestine

sphincter

rectum

anus

The location of the large intestine above the pelvis can be seen on this X-ray image.

large intestine

The large intestine contains trillions of bacteria. Some bacteria help to release vitamins and turn fibre into substances that the body needs. Others help to fight off bad bacteria that can cause illness.

The appendix is a small, thin pouch connected to the large intestine. Scientists are still trying to establish what the appendix is for. Some believe that 'good' bacteria that help with digestion are stored there. Sometimes, the appendix can become inflamed (appendicitis) and may need to be removed.

over 500

the number of species of bacteria in the large intestine

133

Faeces

Faeces is another word for poo, or the solid waste products from the digestive system. Faeces leave the body through an opening called the anus. This is the end of the digestive system.

Faeces form in the large intestine and are stored in the rectum (end of the large intestine) until they are ready to be released. As faeces fill the rectum, the walls of the rectum feel the pressure and send a signal to the brain. When you are ready to go to the toilet, the brain sends a signal to open the sphincter at the base of the rectum so that the faeces can leave the body. Muscles in the anus help to push out the faeces.

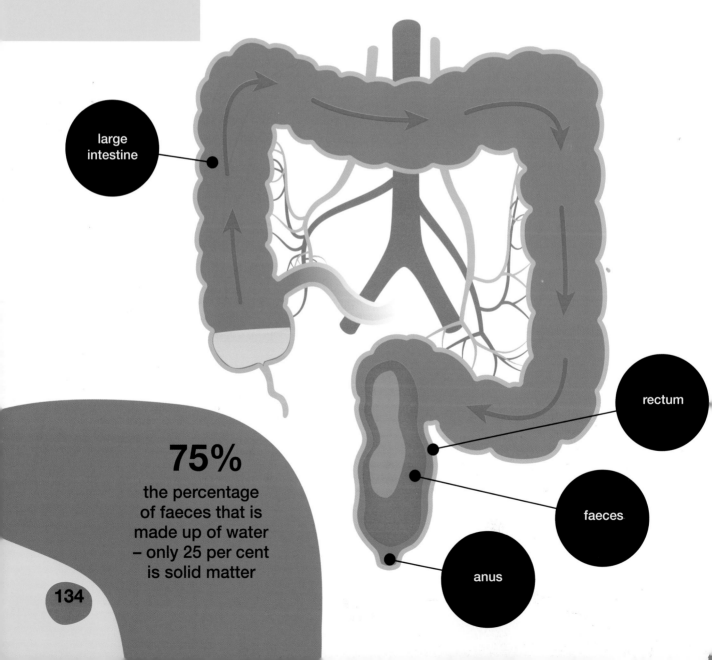

large intestine

rectum

faeces

anus

75%

the percentage of faeces that is made up of water – only 25 per cent is solid matter

The brown colour of faeces comes from bile and dead red blood cells. The smell is due to bacteria. Faeces can come in different forms (see chart below). If you have a healthy digestive system, your faeces should be solid but soft. Constipation or diarrhoea can give your faeces a different appearance.

If you are dehydrated or constipated, too much water is absorbed from the faeces in the large intestine. This makes faeces very dry and hard.

Type 1		Separate hard lumps that are hard to pass
Type 2		A lumpy, hard sausage
Type 3		A sausage with cracks on its surface
Type 4		A smooth, soft sausage
Type 5		Soft blobs with clear edges
Type 6		Fluffy and mushy pieces
Type 7		Liquid, no solid pieces

Your faeces should ideally look like types 3 or 4.

If the intestines are inflamed due to illness, faeces pass through very quickly and come out frequently as watery diarrhoea. This is because the large intestine has not been able to absorb liquid from the faeces.

Constipation can be caused by not eating enough fibre. Eating fibre-rich foods, such as fruit and vegetables, can help to prevent constipation.

The urinary system

As well as faeces, the body also gets rid of urine (liquid waste). Urine passes through its own system as it leaves the body.

Liquids are very important to the body. The average 5–11-year-old should drink 6–8 glasses of liquid (mainly water) a day. Liquid keeps the brain working properly, helps joints to move and flushes away waste products.

Over 50 per cent of blood is liquid water. Water is absorbed into the bloodstream in the large intestine (see pages 132–133). It is carried in the blood to the kidneys, where blood is filtered and excess water, salt and waste products from cells and broken-down proteins are removed. This forms a liquid called urine. Clean blood is sent back around the body through the circulatory system.

kidneys

Urine travels from the kidneys to the bladder along tubes called ureters.

Urine is stored in the bladder. When the bladder is full, it sends a message to the brain that it needs to be emptied. When you go to the toilet, the brain sends a message to sphincters in the bladder, which open.

Muscles in the walls of the bladder push out the urine, which leaves the body through a tube called the urethra.

Doctors often test urine to see if a patient is healthy. Some diseases and conditions, such as diabetes, can cause certain chemicals to be released in urine.

Eating too much of some foods or vitamin pills can turn your urine shocking colours, including neon yellow, bright red and dark brown!

Some medicines and health conditions can change the colour of your urine, too. Talk to an adult or a doctor if you are worried.

bladder

The colour of urine is a good indicator of how much liquid you have drunk.

Transparent or pale yellow urine shows that you are well hydrated.

Dark yellow or brown-orange urine shows that you need to drink more water.

350 ml

the maximum amount of liquid that an adult bladder can hold – around the same amount as an average can of soft drink

Digestive issues

Digestive issues are very common. Most people will experience minor digestive issues, such as constipation, diarrhoea or vomiting at some point in their lives. Other people experience long-term digestive conditions that affect their diet and their everyday lives.

People with coeliac disease can't consume any products that contain gluten, such as bread, pasta, cereal and many pre-prepared foods. However, today there are many gluten-free alternatives for people with coeliac disease, along with naturally gluten-free carbohydrates such as rice and potatoes.

Coeliac disease affects the small intestine. When people with coeliac disease eat a substance called gluten, their immune system mistakenly attacks the gluten when it reaches the small intestine. As a result, the small intestine becomes inflamed and damaged and can't absorb nutrients properly. People with coeliac disease often feel tired because they aren't receiving the nutrients that keep the body healthy. A test can confirm if someone has coeliac disease.

The damage to the villi in the small intestine caused by coeliac disease can be seen in these images (left, a healthy small intestine, and right, someone with coeliac disease).

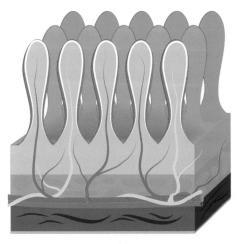

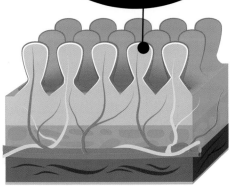

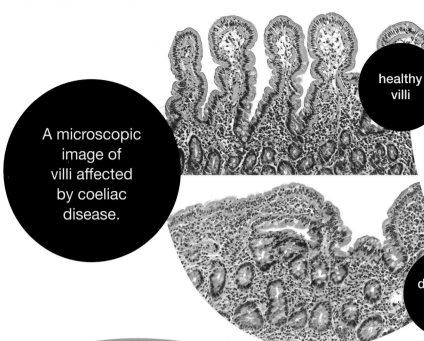

A microscopic image of villi affected by coeliac disease.

healthy villi

damaged villi

1%

the average percentage of the world population with coeliac disease

IBS (irritable bowel syndrome) is a common digestive condition. Its symptoms include bloating, cramps, diarrhoea and constipation. IBS symptoms come and go, or last for days, weeks or even months. Experts haven't yet been able to identify why people suffer from IBS, but stress and certain foods can be triggers.

treatments to manage IBS

relaxation

diet

medicine

gentle exercise such as walking and swimming

symptoms of IBS

bloating

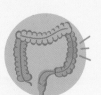
pain

constipation and diarrhoea

mucus in faeces

Types of food

Carbohydrates, proteins and fats are some of the main nutrients that we need to eat as part of a balanced diet. They are digested in different parts of the digestive system and serve many purposes around the body.

- Carbohydrates are found in bread, potatoes, rice, pasta and some fruits. They give the body energy. Complex carbohydrates, such as whole grain bread, provide longer-lasting energy than simple carbohydrates, such as white bread or sugary treats.

- Proteins come from meat, fish, eggs, milk, beans and pulses. They are used to grow and repair cells.

- There are two different types of fat. Saturated fats are found in butter, cheese and processed foods, while unsaturated fats are found in olive oil, nuts, seeds and avocados. Fats are used by the body for energy.

This diagram shows how much of the different food groups you should be eating as part of a balanced diet. Carbohydrates, proteins and fats are found across the different food groups.

Vegetables provide fibre, vitamins and minerals.

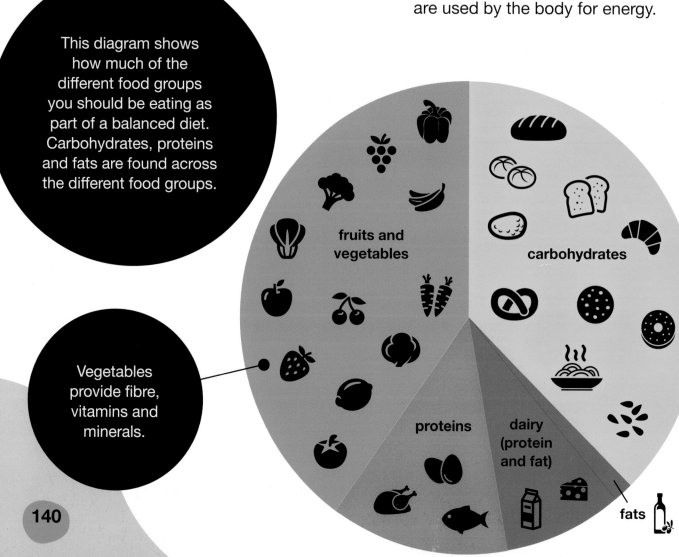

fruits and vegetables

carbohydrates

proteins

dairy (protein and fat)

fats

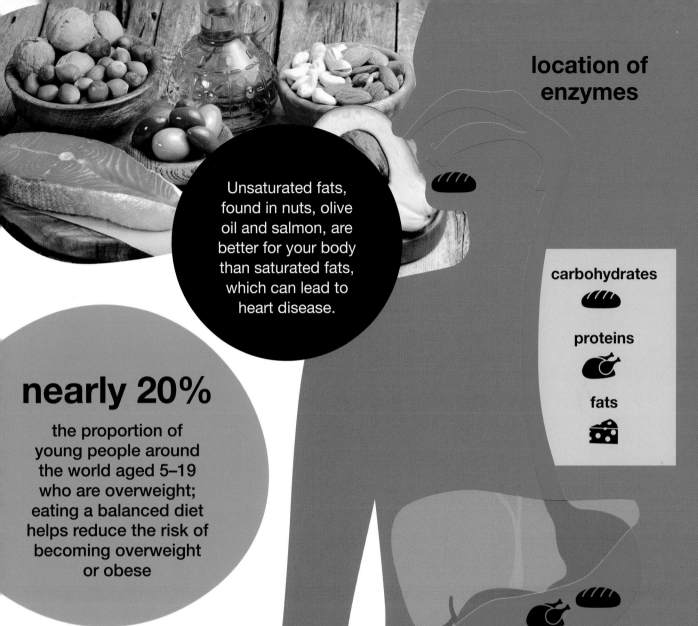

Unsaturated fats, found in nuts, olive oil and salmon, are better for your body than saturated fats, which can lead to heart disease.

carbohydrates

proteins

fats

nearly 20%

the proportion of young people around the world aged 5–19 who are overweight; eating a balanced diet helps reduce the risk of becoming overweight or obese

Different enzymes break down carbohydrates, proteins and fats. The enzymes that break down carbohydrates are released in the mouth, stomach and small intestine. Proteins are broken down by enzymes in the stomach and small intestine. Fats are broken down in the small intestine using bile from the liver (see pages 130–131).

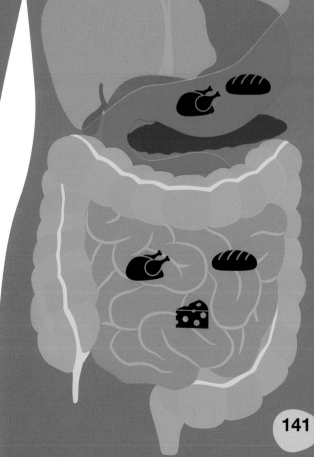

141

Vitamins and minerals

The body needs vitamins and minerals as well as the main food groups to function properly. Only small amounts of vitamins and minerals are needed, but they are very important to the body's overall health.

Below are some of the vitamins and minerals that help to keep the body healthy. If you eat a balanced diet, you are probably consuming all of the vitamins and minerals that you need. However, if you have any dietary restrictions, your doctor may advise you to take supplements.

found in: eggs, meat, vegetables

B vitamins

vitamin A

needed for: improving vision in low light, boosting the immune system and keeping skin healthy

needed for: helping the body release energy from food, supporting the nervous system

found in: dairy products, vegetables

vitamin C

needed for: keeping bones, teeth and muscles healthy

found in: fruit and vegetables, such as oranges and green and red peppers

needed for: protecting cells and keeping them healthy, helping wounds to heal

vitamin D

found in: sunlight, oily fish

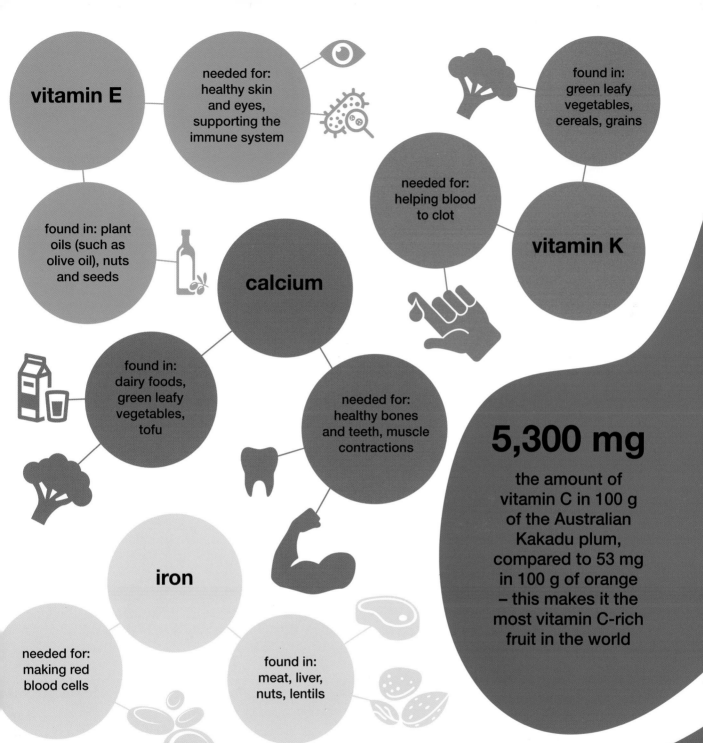

vitamin E

needed for: healthy skin and eyes, supporting the immune system

found in: plant oils (such as olive oil), nuts and seeds

calcium

found in: dairy foods, green leafy vegetables, tofu

needed for: healthy bones and teeth, muscle contractions

found in: green leafy vegetables, cereals, grains

needed for: helping blood to clot

vitamin K

iron

needed for: making red blood cells

found in: meat, liver, nuts, lentils

5,300 mg

the amount of vitamin C in 100 g of the Australian Kakadu plum, compared to 53 mg in 100 g of orange – this makes it the most vitamin C-rich fruit in the world

Seaweed contains more minerals than many land vegetables. It is a source of calcium, iron and iodine, which is needed for chemical reactions in the body.

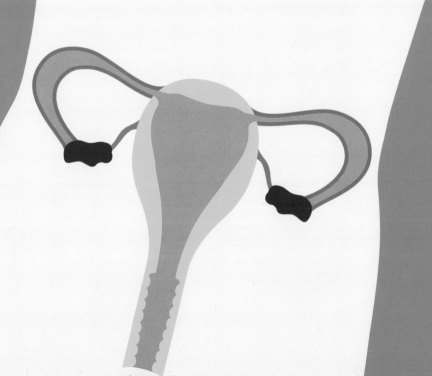

THE REPRODUCTIVE SYSTEM

Reproduction

All living things, from plants to people, can create offspring. This is called reproduction. The parts of the body that allow humans to reproduce make up the reproductive system.

Humans use sexual reproduction to have babies (see pages 162–163). Male and female reproductive systems have different roles in this process. Different reproductive systems are what identify sex as male or female. In this chapter, we will use this wording to describe sex, organs and systems only, which are different to gender. Gender identity has many manifestations and is unique to every person.

The male reproductive system is designed to produce and transport sperm. The main male reproductive organs, the penis and testicles (or testes), are outside the body.

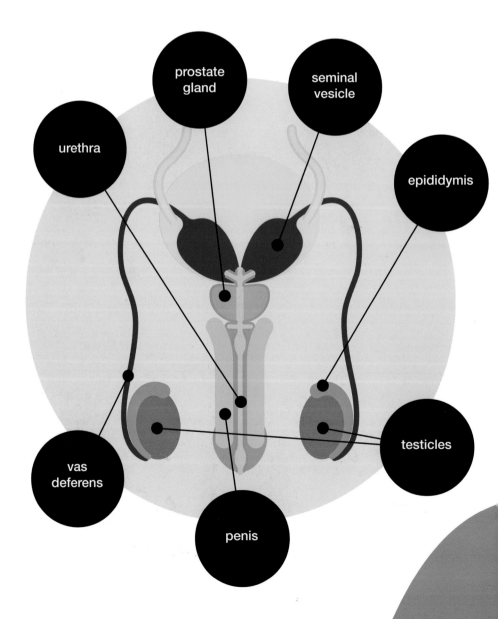

prostate gland

seminal vesicle

urethra

epididymis

vas deferens

testicles

penis

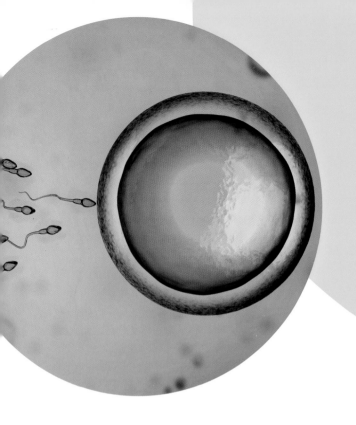

5 micrometres and 120 micrometres

the size of a sperm cell and an egg cell respectively – the smallest and largest cells in the human body

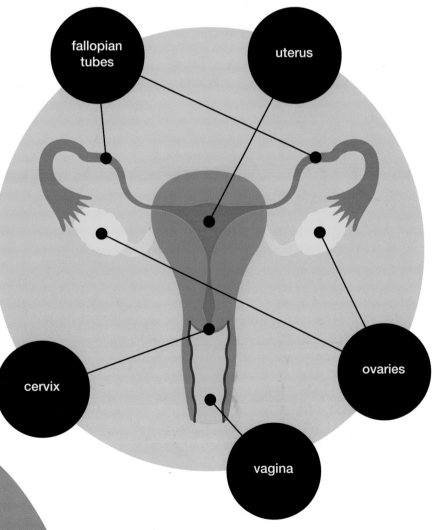

fallopian tubes

uterus

cervix

ovaries

vagina

The female reproductive organs are inside the body. They are designed to conceive a baby and support it as it grows.

Female reproductive organs

The main female body parts involved in reproduction are the ovaries, fallopian tubes, uterus and vagina.

Eggs, or ova, are stored in two ovaries. The eggs in a female system are formed very early on: when a baby is growing inside a uterus. At puberty (see pages 154–155), the ovaries begin releasing an egg about once a month. This process is called ovulation.

The uterus is about the size and shape of a pear. It has strong, muscular walls that stretch as a baby grows inside it.

The fallopian tubes connect the ovaries to the uterus.

The vagina is a muscular tube that sperm travels through during sexual reproduction. The baby passes through the vagina during childbirth.

Two ovaries in the lower stomach area contain the eggs.

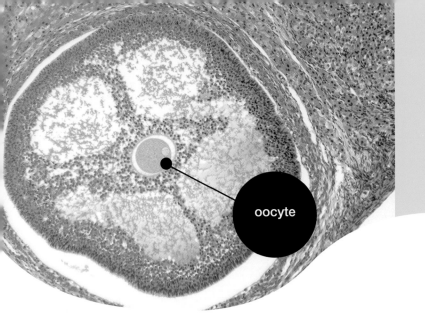

This microscopic image shows a developing egg cell, called an oocyte. The female system has between 1 and 2 million eggs at birth, but thousands die before adulthood.

oocyte

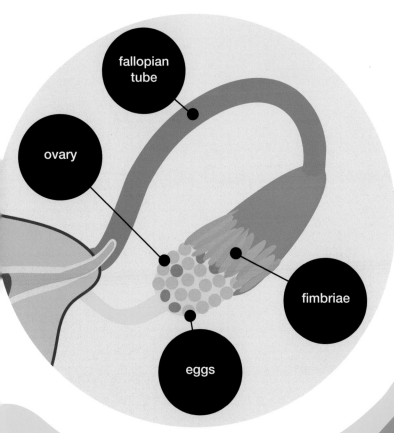

fallopian tube

ovary

fimbriae

eggs

The finger-like extensions on the fallopian tubes are called fimbriae. These scoop up the egg from the surface of the ovary and move it into the fallopian tube.

12 cm

the approximate length of a fallopian tube; each one is as thin as a needle

Male reproductive organs

The main male body parts involved in reproduction are the penis and testicles, as well as three glands called the prostate and the seminal vesicles.

A coiled tube behind the testicles, called the epididymis, stores sperm and transports it from the testicles.

Semen is the fluid that, after puberty, contains sperm. It is produced after puberty in two oval-shaped glands called testicles.

The vas deferens are tubes that lead from the testicles to the seminal vesicles.

During sexual reproduction, sperm passes through the penis into the vagina.

The testicles are held in a pouch of skin called the scrotum.

150

There are three parts to the penis: the root, the shaft (body) and the glans. The root attaches the penis to the wall of the abdomen. The shaft is shaped like a cylinder. It is made up of three chambers of spongy tissue. During sexual arousal, these chambers fill with blood, making the penis erect. The glans is the head of the penis. It is covered with a layer of loose skin called the foreskin, unless the foreskin is removed through circumcision for religious or medical reasons, or parental preference.

The prostate gland and the seminal vesicles produce some of the fluid in semen.

525 billion

the average number of sperm cells produced in the lifetime of a male system

glans

shaft

root

Hormones and reproduction

Hormones are special chemicals in the body. They control our moods and metabolism, how we grow, the way our organs work, and many other things. Hormones play an important part in the reproductive system, and are different in male and female systems.

Hormones are made in glands all over the body. Each gland controls different things. Together, these glands make up the endocrine system.

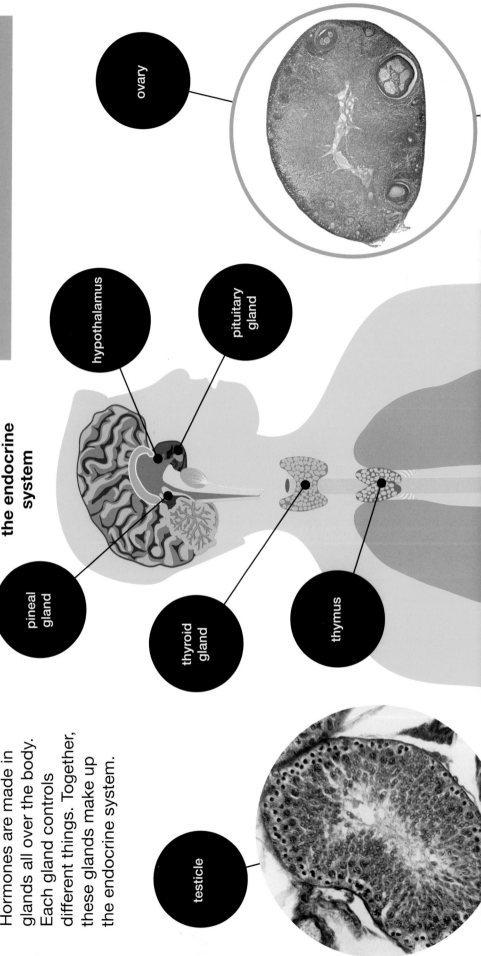

ovary

hypothalamus

pituitary gland

the endocrine system

pineal gland

thyroid gland

thymus

testicle

The hormones oestrogen and progesterone come from the ovaries.

pancreas

adrenal glands

ovaries (female system)

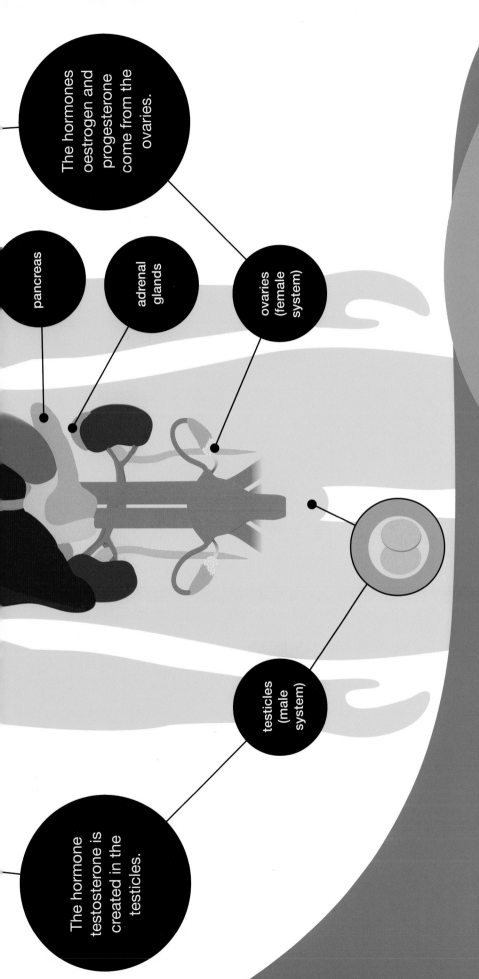

testicles (male system)

The hormone testosterone is created in the testicles.

1,460–2,555 milligrams

the amount of testosterone produced in an average male system each year – that's one-third to half a teaspoon

The hormones produced by the reproductive organs control secondary sexual characteristics. These are things other than the reproductive organs that are different in male and female bodies. For example, facial hair and breasts.

153

Female puberty

The reproductive organs usually start to release hormones a year or two before the teenage years. This causes the start of puberty – a time when the body matures and becomes capable of sexual reproduction.

Female puberty may begin any time between the ages of eight and fourteen. During puberty, the body changes size and shape. One of these changes is a growth spurt in height, up to 7.5 cm in a year.

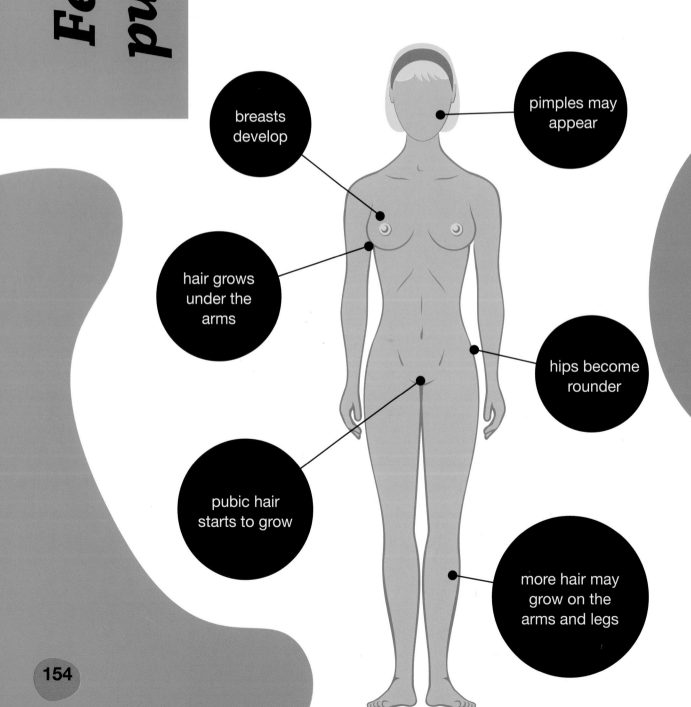

breasts develop

pimples may appear

hair grows under the arms

hips become rounder

pubic hair starts to grow

more hair may grow on the arms and legs

Acne is a common skin condition among teenagers. It appears as spots on the face, back or torso.

During puberty, hormones make the glands in the skin create more of an oily substance called sebum. This can mix with dead skin and block hair follicles, causing spots. Blackheads appear on the surface of the skin. Whiteheads form just beneath the surface.

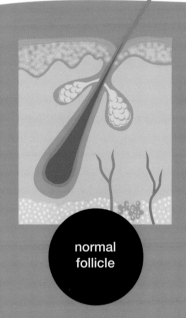

normal follicle

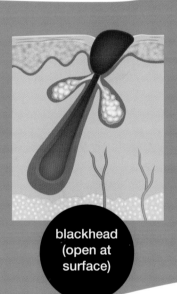

blackhead (open at surface)

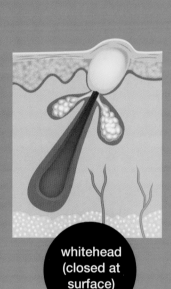

whitehead (closed at surface)

About two years after female puberty starts, menstruation begins (see pages 156–157). This means the body is technically able to bear children. However, it would be physically dangerous to have a child at this age, and it may be many years before the person is mentally ready to have a baby.

4 years

the length of time puberty usually lasts in a female system

The menstrual cycle

Pregnancy is possible because of a process called the menstrual cycle. This is a series of changes that takes place each month in the female reproductive system.

The eggs that are present in the female system at birth are 'immature'. That means they are not fully developed. Eggs mature when they are needed to become part of the menstrual cycle. An egg cannot be fertilised (see pages 164–165) until it has been released from an ovary.

Once an egg has been released by an ovary, it passes through the fallopian tube to the uterus. If an egg is unfertilised when it reaches the uterus, it will continue on its journey towards the vagina. Eventually, the egg leaves the body, along with the extra lining that the uterus does not need. This bleeding is commonly known as a period.

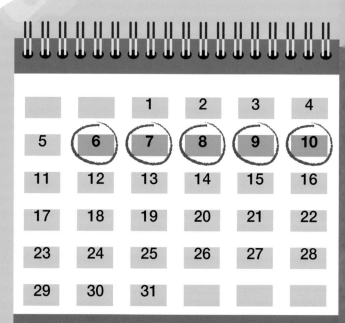

The whole menstrual cycle takes an average of 28 days. A period usually lasts for about five days.

30–40 millilitres

the average amount of blood passed during a period (that's 2–3 tablespoons)

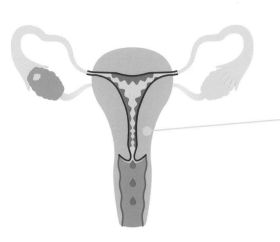

0–7 days
The inner lining of the uterus is shed from the previous cycle.

Menstrual blood passes out of the body.

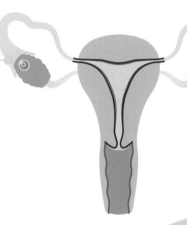

8–11 days
The egg begins to mature in the ovary.

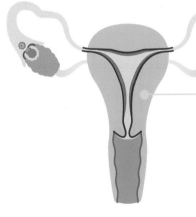

12–16 days
Ovulation takes place – the egg moves out of the ovary into the fallopian tube.

The uterus begins to prepare for pregnancy: the lining grows thicker with extra blood and tissue.

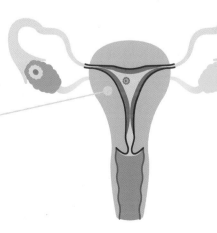

17–28 days
The egg is released into the uterus and travels through it.

Male puberty

Male puberty begins a bit later than female puberty – usually around the age of twelve. However, puberty can begin at any time between the ages of eight and fourteen. It usually ends between sixteen and eighteen years of age.

As during female puberty, male puberty produces many changes, including height growth spurts – up to 7–8 cm in a year. The muscles also grow, especially around the arms, legs and torso.

facial hair grows

spots may appear

pubic hair grows

underarm hair grows

glands release hormones that cause increased sweating

penis and testicles grow larger

Testosterone typically causes facial hair to start growing towards the end of puberty, although it may be thin to begin with.

During puberty, the voice 'breaks', which means it becomes permanently lower. This happens after the testicles and penis have gone through a growth spurt. It is caused by testosterone affecting how the larynx (voice box) grows. The vocal cords get thicker so they can't vibrate as quickly. This makes the voice lower.

2–4 million

the number of sweat glands in the human body

An Adam's apple appears during male puberty. This lump in the neck is made of cartilage surrounding the larynx.

As well as external changes, internal developments are also going on during male puberty. For instance, this is when the body starts producing sperm.

The hormone testosterone stimulates the production of sperm cells. These are created in the testicles. From puberty onwards, the male system produces millions of sperm cells every day.

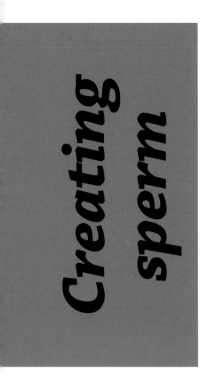

Testosterone turns special cells into sperm inside tubes in the testicles.

The sperm enter the epididymis, where they complete their development.

The mature sperm pass into the vas deferens (see page 146).

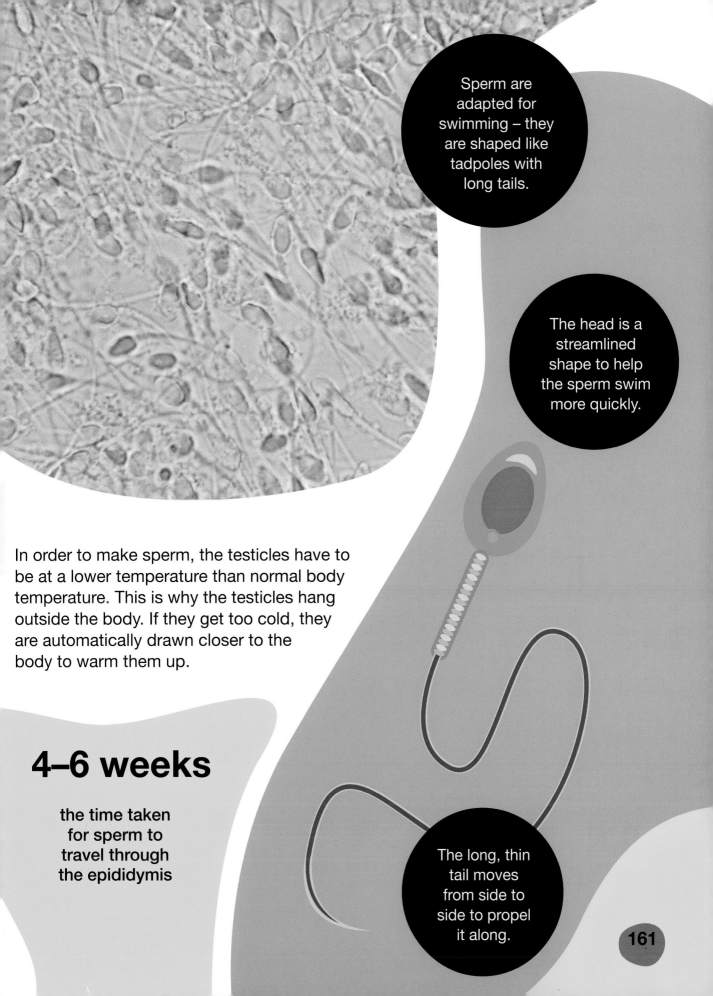

Sperm are adapted for swimming – they are shaped like tadpoles with long tails.

The head is a streamlined shape to help the sperm swim more quickly.

In order to make sperm, the testicles have to be at a lower temperature than normal body temperature. This is why the testicles hang outside the body. If they get too cold, they are automatically drawn closer to the body to warm them up.

4–6 weeks

the time taken for sperm to travel through the epididymis

The long, thin tail moves from side to side to propel it along.

Sexual reproduction and inheritance

All mammals, including humans, reproduce sexually. During sexual reproduction, a male sex cell and a female sex cell join together.

During sex, the penis releases semen into the vagina. The semen contains millions of sperm cells. The sperm cells pass through the vagina and into the uterus. From there, they swim up the fallopian tubes. If they meet an egg, fertilisation may occur (see pages 164–165). When fertilisation takes place, a zygote is formed.

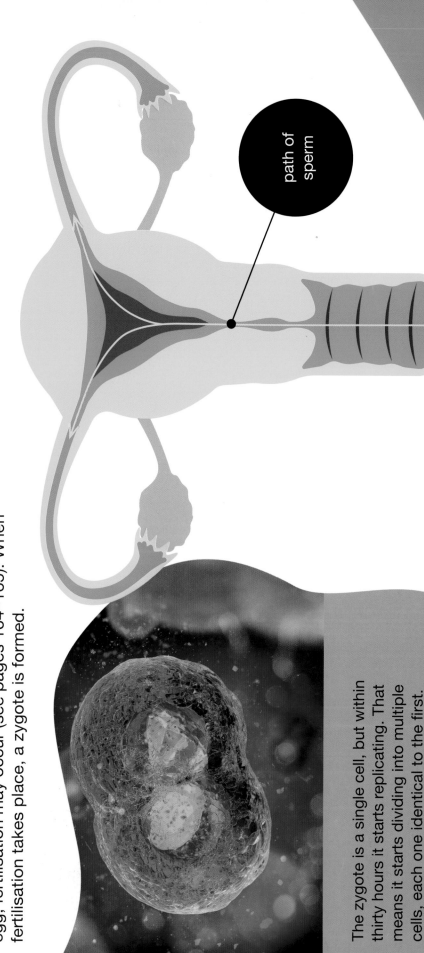

path of sperm

The zygote is a single cell, but within thirty hours it starts replicating. That means it starts dividing into multiple cells, each one identical to the first.

36

the lifespan in hours of a sperm cell

Chromosomes are tiny structures inside cells. They carry lots of information about you. Some of that information is about your inheritance characteristics, such as your hair and eye colour.

During sexual reproduction, these join to create a zygote. This has 46 chromosomes, like a normal human cell.

Every cell in your body has 46 chromosomes, divided into pairs. But sex cells are different.

The egg cell contains 23 chromosomes.

The sperm cell contains 23 chromosomes.

For a baby to be created, fertilisation must take place. Fertilisation is when a sperm cell enters an egg cell.

Fertilisation occurs in the longest and widest part of the fallopian tube. The sperm can reach the egg here. Only one sperm is able to enter an egg, but that is enough for fertilisation to take place.

The sperm head releases a special substance that breaks down the outer layer of the egg.

The sperm head enters the egg.

Lots of sperm try to penetrate the egg.

A fertilisation membrane forms around the egg to stop any more sperm entering once a sperm cell has entered.

Once fertilised, the egg continues on its journey down the fallopian tube. Along the way, it divides into more cells. Eventually, it enters the uterus. It buries itself in the lining of the uterus and begins to grow.

Day 1: fertilisation

Day 2: divides into two cells

Day 2: divides again into four cells

Day 3: divides into eight cells

Day 6: ball of multiple cells enters the uterus

Day 5: divides into sixteen cells

12–24 hours

the lifespan of an egg once it has been released from the ovary

The cluster of cells that eventually enters the uterus is known as a blastocyst.

Pregnancy

Pregnancy lasts for nine months. The baby grows very quickly in size during this time, from smaller than a grain of sand, to an infant weighing about 3.5 kg.

Between fertilisation and eight weeks, the blastocyst is known as an embryo. At this stage, the cells in the embryo become specialised. This means that they develop to perform certain functions in the body, by transforming into cells such as nerve cells. From eight weeks to birth, the baby is called a foetus. This stage is about growth and development.

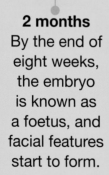

1 month
The blastocyst has become an embryo.

2 months
By the end of eight weeks, the embryo is known as a foetus, and facial features start to form.

3 months
The baby measures about 5 cm.

4 months
The heart is fully formed.

5 months
The baby may suck its thumb, yawn and stretch inside the uterus.

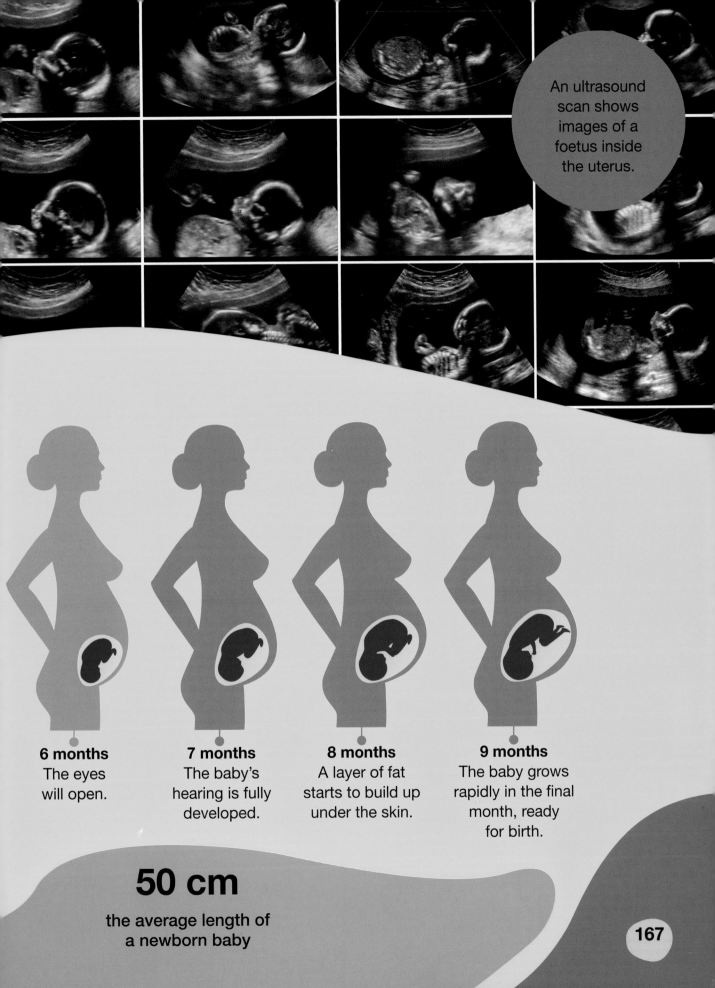

An ultrasound scan shows images of a foetus inside the uterus.

6 months
The eyes will open.

7 months
The baby's hearing is fully developed.

8 months
A layer of fat starts to build up under the skin.

9 months
The baby grows rapidly in the final month, ready for birth.

50 cm
the average length of a newborn baby

Multiple births

Most of the time just one egg is fertilised, and it grows into a single baby. But that's not always the case. Sometimes people have two (twins), three (triplets) or even more babies in a single pregnancy.

There are different types of twins. Identical twins are the result of a zygote (see page 162) splitting into two separate zygotes. This happens within fourteen days of fertilisation. Because they come from a single egg, the babies will be the same sex and will have exactly the same genetic make-up.

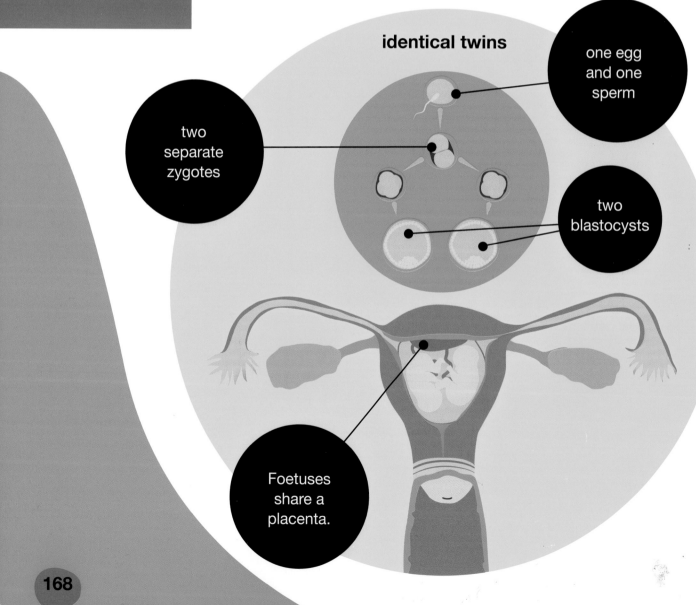

identical twins

one egg and one sperm

two separate zygotes

two blastocysts

Foetuses share a placenta.

Sometimes, two eggs are released from the ovaries at the same time. If two separate sperm fertilise these two separate eggs, non-identical twins will be conceived. These twins may be very like each other – or they may be very different! It is not uncommon for them to be different sexes.

non-identical twins

two eggs and two sperm

two blastocysts

Usually, each foetus has its own placenta.

Triplets can form in two ways. A zygote may split evenly into three parts, forming three separate zygotes. Or, a zygote may split in two, and then one of those parts may split again.

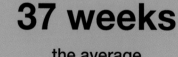

37 weeks

the average length of a twin pregnancy – three weeks less than a typical pregnancy

Infertility

The reproductive system does not always work in the way it should. Some people may have difficulty getting pregnant. This might be because either person has low fertility or is infertile.

A male system may have a low sperm count, which means it produces fewer sperm than usual. Sometimes sperm cells can be damaged so they do not function properly.

An example of a normal sperm count (left) vs a lower sperm count.

A female system may have a blockage in a fallopian tube, or ovulation may not occur.

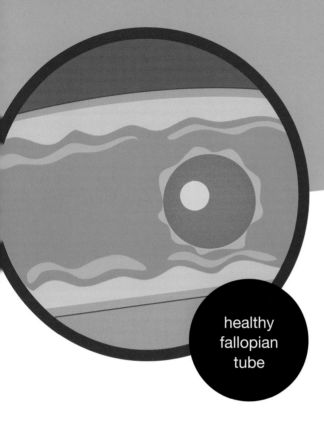

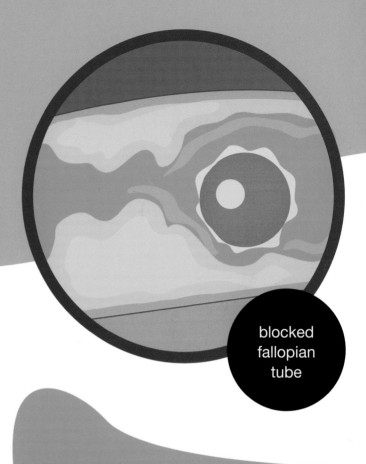

blocked fallopian tube

healthy fallopian tube

In vitro fertilisation (IVF) can help infertile people get pregnant. During IVF, an egg is removed from an ovary and fertilised with a sperm in a laboratory. Doctors then implant the already fertilised egg in a uterus.

Although an egg is fertilised outside the body in IVF, once implanted in the uterus, it grows and develops like a embryo that has been conceived naturally.

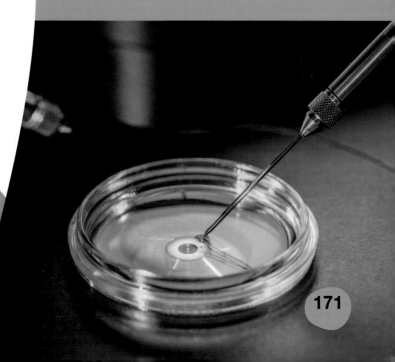

1 in 7

the number of couples who have difficulty getting pregnant naturally

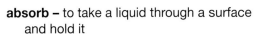
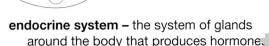

Glossary

absorb – to take a liquid through a surface and hold it

aerobic respiration – the process in which cells use oxygen to produce energy from food

alveoli – very small air sacs in the lungs where gas exchange takes place

amplitude – the distance from the rest position to the top of a sound wave

antibody – something that sticks to pathogens and destroys them

anus – the opening through which faeces leave the body

artery – a blood vessel that carries blood from the heart to other parts of the body

biceps – the muscles at the front of the upper arm

bile – a substance produced by the liver that breaks down fat in the small intestine

binocular vision – the combined, overlapping sight from two eyes that allows us to see objects in depth

bloodstream – the flow of blood around the body

bolus – a ball of chewed food in the mouth or oesophagus

bone marrow – the spongy centre of long bones, where blood is made

capillary – a very thin blood vessel

carbon dioxide – a waste gas produced by cells during aerobic respiration

cardiovascular system – the system of the heart and blood vessels

cartilage – a strong tissue between bones that stops them grinding together

cell – the smallest living part of a living thing

central nervous system – the brain and spinal cord

chyme – a mushy liquid of broken-down food, found in the stomach and intestines

clot – to turn from a liquid into a solid lump

compact – when something is dense and closely packed together

conceive – to successfully create an embryo

diaphragm – the large band of muscle between the lungs and the stomach

effector – a part of the body that produces a response, such as a muscle or a gland

embryo – an unborn child in the first eight weeks of pregnancy

endocrine system – the system of glands around the body that produces hormones

enzyme – a chemical that helps to break down substances, such as food

femur – the long thigh bone, between the hip and the knee

fimbriae – long, thin projections at the end of the fallopian tube

flexible – describes something that can bend in lots of different ways

foetus – the name for an unborn child after the eighth week of pregnancy

foreskin – a piece of loose skin that covers the penis

gene – a part of a living thing's DNA that is passed on from its parents and which controls different qualities, such as hair colour or blood group

gland – an organ that produces and releases substances in the body

haemoglobin – a substance in red blood cells that binds to oxygen and carries it around the body

hormone – a chemical that controls important processes in the body

immune system – the cells and systems in the body that protect it from disease

inheritance – characteristics that may be passed on from parents to children

internal – inside the body

involuntary – describes an action that you cannot control

larynx – the voice box

lobe – an area of the brain or lungs

mammals – a group of warm-blooded animals, including humans, characterised by having hair or fur, the females making milk to feed their young and (with a few exceptions) giving birth to live young

membrane – a thin layer of tissue

metabolism – chemical reactions in cells that create energy to power everything we do

micrometre – one millionth of a metre (one thousandth of a millimetre)

minerals – natural substances that help the body grow and stay healthy

molecule – the smallest unit of a substance

motor neurone – a nerve cell that carries signals from the central nervous system to effectors

neurone – a nerve cell

nutrient – a substance that a living thing needs to grow and be healthy

odour – a smell

oesophagus – the tube that connects the mouth to the stomach

organ – an important part of the body that performs a specific function, such as the heart and lungs

ovulation – the process in which an egg is released from the ovary into the fallopian tube

oxygen – a gas found in the air that cells need to produce energy

papillae – bumps on the tongue that contain taste buds

paralysis – a condition where someone is unable to move all or part of the body, caused by damage to the nervous system

pathogen – a very small organism that can cause disease, such as a virus or bacteria

pelvis – the large frame of bone at the bottom of the spine, which the legs are attached to

peripheral nervous system – the nerves around the body that connect to the central nervous system

peristalsis – muscular movement that pushes material along

pitch – how high or low a sound is

plasma – a liquid that forms 54 per cent of human blood

platelets – cells in the blood that clot at a wound to stop blood from escaping

proprioception – the sense of the position and strength of the body

receptor – a specialised cell that senses changes in the environment

reflex – a quick, involuntary response to stimuli

relay neurone – a nerve cell that carries signals within the central nervous system

respiratory system – the system of the airways and lungs

saliva – spit

sebum – an oily substance created in the sebaceous glands of the skin

semen – the fluid that contains sperm after puberty

sensory neurone – a nerve cell that carries signals from receptors to the central nervous system

sensory neurone – a nerve cell that carries signals from receptors to the central nervous system

spasm – a sudden, rapid involuntary movement of a muscle

sphincter – a circular muscle that opens and closes

spinal cord – a long, thin tube inside the bones in the spine that contains billions of neurones

sternum – a flat bone at the front of the chest

stimuli (a stimulus) – something that causes part of the body to react

synovial fluid – a liquid that surrounds joints to help them move smoothly

trachea – the tube that carries air from the top of the throat to the lungs

triceps – the muscles at the back of the upper arm

unconscious – describes something that happens without you being aware of it

vein – a blood vessel that carries blood to the heart from other parts of the body

vertebrae – the bones that make up the column of the spine

zygote – the earliest stage of a fertilised egg

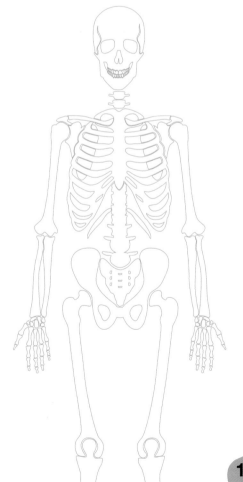

173

Index

First published in Great Britain in 2021 by Wayland

Copyright © Hodder & Stoughton Limited, 2021

 Original series produced for Wayland by
White-Thomson Publishing Ltd
www.wtpub.co.uk

Editors: John Hort and Grace Glendinning
Cover Design: Thy Bui
Designer: Dan Prescott, Couper Street Type Co.

HB ISBN: 978 1 5263 1660 8
10 9 8 7 6 5 4 3 2 1

Wayland
An imprint of Hachette Children's Group
Part of Hodder & Stoughton
Carmelite House
50 Victoria Embankment
London EC4Y 0DZ

An Hachette UK Company
www.hachette.co.uk
www.hachettechildrens.co.uk

Printed in China

MIX
Paper from
responsible sources
FSC® C104740
www.fsc.org

The material in this book has previously been published in the following titles:
The Bright and Bold Human Body: The Brain and Nervous System
The Bright and Bold Human Body: The Digestive System
The Bright and Bold Human Body: The Heart, Lungs and Blood
The Bright and Bold Human Body: The Reproductive System
The Bright and Bold Human Body: The Senses
The Bright and Bold Human Body: The Skeleton and Muscles

Picture credits:

Alamy: Science Photo Library 45 and 80b; Science Picture Co 51.

Getty Images: Ed Reschke 57r.

Science Photo Library: Steve Gschmeissner 75t, 97r; Susumu Nishinaga 61b.

Istock: Nerthuz 41b; BahadirTanriover 42l; Maartje van Caspel 47t; Ogphoto 52t; PeterHermesFurian 55t; normaals 55b and 96; yodiyim 65b; ttsz 69t, 75b, 79, 103t, 128 and 138b; K_E_N 69b; ericsphotography 72b; colematt 73; ElizabethHoffmann 77b; Vector Mine 96; Tetiana, kowalska-art 125b, Rost-9D 131b.

Shutterstock: Lemberg Vector studio 8, 9l, 18, and 124; stanga 9r; joshya 11t and 151; Crevis 11b; NoPainNoGain 12; vetpathologist 13; Artemida-psy 14,171t; Studio BKK 15; udaix 16–17,18, 50–51; Ellen Bronstayn 17l; Puwadol Jaturawutthichai 17r; ellepicgrafica 18; Designua 20, 26, 27t, 48, 57l, 74, 76, 77c, 78t, 80t, 103t, 105t, 111r, 149b, 152–153,164; itsmejust 21t; elenabsl 21b, 52b, 53,123b; Helena Ohman 22; Bizroug 23t; VectorMine 23b, 30, 44, 60, 64–65, 68, 72t, 81, 100, 107, 114t, 146, 147b, 157 and 165t; Macrovector 24–25, 36–37c; Tinydevil 25; snapgalleria 27b; Benjamin Ordaz 28; Scalapendra 29t;Dmitry Yashkin 29b; Andrey_Popov 31; Luis Santos 32b: Aksanaku 32t, 33t, 33b; Tomacco 36r; Richman Photo 37r; Luciano Cosmo 38,154; Jose Luis Calvo 39, 70b,123t; cash1994 40; NotionPic 41t; gritsalak karalak 45t, 55c,102,117,129t, 161b; MadPierre 49b;ShadeDesign 54; corbac 40, 56–57c; TippaPatt 59; ellepigrafica 61t,110, 121t; Asmus Koefoed 66; BigMouse 67; ducu59us 70t; Alila Medical Media 71, 86t and 150; Sakurra 75tr, 93r, 97l; jehsomwang 77t, 92; BigBlueStudio 78b; Suiraton 82; decade3d - anatomy online 83; pixelheadphoto digitalskillet 85t,169b; Blamb 85b,122; nokwalai 86b; metamorworks 90, 141r; mimagephotography 91; Johanna Goodyear 93tl; Helenabdullah 93bl; Peter Hermes Furian 93c; pathdoc 95t; Kzenon 99t; trgrowth 99b; Rocketclips Inc 101t,121b; solar22 104; puhhha 105b; Dario Lo Presti 106; Nina Puankova 108; Juriah Mosin 109b; Giovanni Cancemi 111l; Panda Vector 112t; shopplaywood 112l; Pszczola 112r; YanLev 113t; eveleen 113b,118; ARZTSAMUI 114b; Lisovskaya Natalia 119; UGREEN 3S 125b; siam.pukkato 127; Syda Productions 129b;Tefi 131t; Marochkina Anastasiia 132,134; MriMan 133; Elena Veselova 135b; Vecton 136,163l; Nasky 137l; Guschenkova 137r; margouillat photo 138t; David Litman 139t; Irina Strelnikova 139b; Craevschii Family 141l; maramorosz 143b; koya979 147t; BlueRingMedia 148; Kateryna Kon 149t, 153t,165b; Choksawatdikorn 153b; Itummy 155t; Teguh Mujiono 155b; Makyzz 156; naum 158; Pavel L Photo and Video 159t; Only background 159b; GraphicsRF 160; Lukasz Pawel Szczepanski 161t; Andrii Vodolazhskyi 163r; Ody_Stocker 162; VikiVector 166–167; Gagliardilmages 167t; Veronika Zakharova 168,169t; Logika600 170; MidoSemsem 171b; Techtype115, 126,135t.

All design elements from Shutterstock.

Every effort has been made to clear copyright. Should there be any inadvertent omission, please apply to the publisher for rectification.